MW00563500

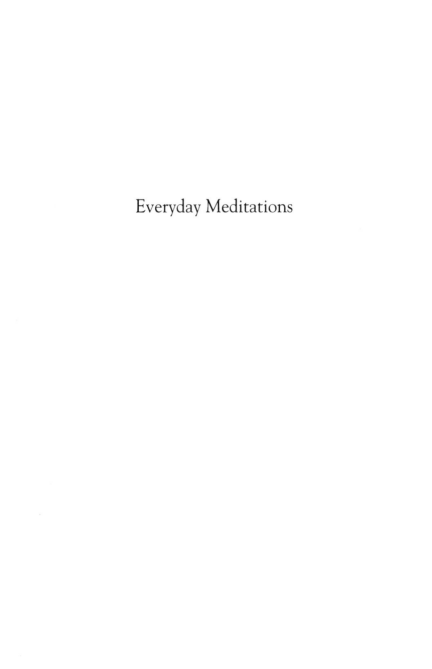

Everyday Meditations

"Blessed John Henry Newman is remembered for the brilliance of his mind and the persuasive power of his writing. But above all, Newman touches the heart. He wins the reader with clarity and beauty, as evidenced on every page of this wonderful book. His work is a labor of joy; it changes us for the better. *Everyday Meditations* is the kind of book that, if taken to heart, draws us into the arms of God."

+Charles J. Chaput, O.F.M. Cap.
Archbishop of Philadelphia

John Henry Newman

Everyday Meditations

SOPHIA INSTITUTE PRESS
Manchester, New Hampshire

Everyday Meditations is taken from the section "Meditations on Christian Doctrine" in *Meditations and Devotions of the Late Cardinal Newman*, published by Longmans, Green, and Company, London, in 1916. This 2013 book by Sophia Institute Press includes minor editorial revisions and a new introduction.

Sophia Institute Press
Box 5284, Manchester, NH 03108
1-800-888-9344

www.SophiaInstitute.com

Sophia Institute Press® is a registered trademark of Sophia Institute.

Library of Congress Cataloging-in-Publication Data

Newman, John Henry, 1801-1890.
    [Meditations and devotions of the late Cardinal Newman.]
    Everyday meditations / John Henry Newman.
      pages cm
    ISBN 978-1-933184-96-8 (pbk. : alk. paper) 1. Meditations.
    2. Catholic Church — Doctrines — Meditations. I. Title.
    BX2182.3.N45 2013
    242'.2 — dc23

                                    2013004087

Contents

Introduction

Blessed John Henry Newman:
A Teacher of Everyday Conversion

by Bishop James D. Conley

Blessed John Henry Newman has a way of changing lives. Perhaps he has already changed yours in some way. Or perhaps he soon will, through these *Everyday Meditations*.

Newman's influence on my life is profound. His writings drew me into the Church as a young college student and helped me discern my priestly vocation.

Whether you are a newcomer to Newman, or a long-time reader of his works, you will find treasure in these devotional writings of England's most illustrious Catholic convert.

It is possible to appreciate these meditations without knowing Newman's own story. His love of the Lord speaks for itself on every page. But John Henry Newman's life is an inspiring piece of Catholic history, and it always helps to be acquainted, or reacquainted, with the person we take as our spiritual guide.

* * *

John Henry Newman was born in 1801, the son of a banker and the oldest of six children. Born into a century of skepticism, John questioned the Bible and doubted the immortality of the soul. The young Newman had a yearning for truth—but this passion was tainted with pride. His pride led him into serious doubts and even the "deliberate rejection of God's voice."

But at age fifteen he underwent a dramatic Christian conversion, recounted in one of this volume's meditations:

> O my God, that overpowering love took me captive. Was any boyhood so impious as some years of mine! Did I not in fact dare you to do your worst? Ah, how I struggled to get free from you; but you are stronger than I and have prevailed. I have not a word to say, but to bow down in awe before the depths of your love.

The young Newman became a fervent evangelical Christian. But he had not yet found the fullness of faith and truth: "In course of time, slowly but infallibly did your grace bring me on into your Church."

Feeling called to ministry, Newman was ordained in the Anglican Communion in 1825. He abandoned low-church evangelicalism, embracing liturgical worship and the early Church Fathers. During the 1830s, he spearheaded the "Oxford Movement," recovering many ancient Christian traditions.

But was Anglicanism, with its sixteenth-century Protestant roots, really "the Church"? By 1841, Newman was no longer sure. After all, Christ's Church was no human invention. Its teachings were not a matter of personal interpretation. As Newman reflected in a later meditation: "The Church is your work, your establishment, your instrument. . . . We are under your rule, your laws and your eye. . . . When the Church speaks you do speak."

Only the Catholic Church spoke with Christ's authoritative voice. In 1845, after writing his Essay on the Development of Christian Doctrine, Newman left Anglicanism and became a Catholic.

Newman's Catholic conversion was the fruit of much thought and prayer, but it was also—like his youthful Christian conversion—an unmerited gift of God's grace:

I adore you, almighty Lord ... because you in your infinite compassion have brought me into this Church, the work of your supernatural power. I had no claim on you for so wonderful a favor over anyone else in the whole world. There were many men far better than I.... Yet you, in your inscrutable love for me, have chosen me and brought me into your fold.

He asked God to make him worthy of this gift:

Now then give me this further grace, Lord, to use all this grace well and to turn it to my salvation.... Give me a love of your sacraments and ordinances.... Without you I can do nothing, and you are there where your Church is and your sacraments.

Newman was ordained a Catholic priest in 1846 and joined the Oratory of St. Philip Neri. Over the next four decades, he undertook various pastoral and intellectual works—including an apostolate among the poor and the foundation of Ireland's first Catholic university. Although his life as a Catholic priest was challenging, he never doubted his choice to join "the one fold of the redeemer."

Blessed John Henry Newman lived to see his achievements honored, especially through his 1879 appointment as a cardinal. Since his death in 1890, his reputation as a priest and author has only grown.

A Teacher of Everyday Conversion

* * *

Cardinal Newman is known for his theological writings, which strengthened the Church's intellectual credibility in the modern world. He foresaw the rise of relativism—the belief that individuals can have "their own truth"—and fought it on many fronts. His arguments for the Catholic Faith have inspired many conversions, including mine.

But Newman did not set out to be a public intellectual. His goal in life was something much simpler—and harder. John Henry Newman's goal was to imitate and proclaim Jesus Christ; to serve God and love his neighbor as himself; to know the Lord and make him known.

It is this side of Newman, his heart as a disciple and preacher that we encounter in these *Everyday Meditations*. Here we discover Newman as the teacher of a different kind of conversion: the ongoing growth in sanctity to which Christ's faithful are constantly called.

All of us need this "everyday conversion"—no matter how well we know our Faith or how long we have practiced it. This deepening of faith and love is sometimes known as the "second conversion." It builds upon our initial reception of grace in Baptism.

The *Catechism of the Catholic Church* describes the "second conversion" as "an uninterrupted task for the whole Church" (CCC 1428). This everyday conversion draws us more deeply into the mystery of Christ, joining our lives to his in every way.

To follow Jesus completely, we must undergo both of these "conversions": the initial acceptance of truth and the lifelong process of transformation by the Holy Spirit. John Henry Newman is a wise and kindly guide for those undertaking this journey of deeper conversion—just as he is for those first finding their way to the one Church of Christ.

* * *

Even after he had become a Catholic, Newman understood his need for continual conversion. Like his initial turn toward Christ in adolescence, his midlife reception into the Church was the beginning of a journey—not the end.

As a Catholic, John Henry Newman could rely on the Church's teaching authority in faith and morals. He could rest assured that the Church taught the truth in these matters, but he also understood the need for a close, personal relationship with God, the need to walk closely with him in his daily life—hearing the voice of Christ not only through the teachings of the Church, but also in the depths of his own heart and soul. Newman, a brilliant teacher of the Faith, could still look to Jesus and declare: "I need you to teach me day by day, according to each day's opportunities and needs."

> Teach me ... to sit at your feet and to hear your word. Give me that true wisdom which seeks your will by prayer and meditation.... Give me the discernment to know your voice from the voice of strangers, and to rest upon it and to seek it in the first place.

Christian discipleship must be founded on truth—and this means looking to the Catholic Church as the "pillar and ground of truth." Even then, however, there is no substitute for our own direct relationship with the Lord. Our acceptance of Church teaching will profit us little if we do not seek God—and find him—in our daily lives.

This is the work of the "second conversion." It requires daily prayer, good works, and reverent reception of the sacraments. And spiritual reading—time spent with works such as these meditations by Newman—also plays an important role in this process.

* * *

John Henry Newman was a brilliant thinker, but he is not "blessed" on that account. He is numbered among the blessed because he loved God in purity of heart and helped others to do the same.

I hope this volume will help the Church appreciate Newman's legacy, not only as a thinker, but as a priest, preacher, and disciple.

Above all, I hope these writings will change your life. I hope they will speak to your heart—helping you grow in faith, hope, and love. That is their purpose and their blessed author's intention.

Everyday Meditations

A Prayer before Meditation

I place myself in the presence of him in whose Incarnate Presence I am before I place myself there.

I adore you, O my Savior, present here as God and man, in soul and body, in true flesh and blood.

I acknowledge and confess that I kneel before that Sacred Humanity, which was conceived in Mary's womb and lay in Mary's bosom, which grew up to man's estate, and by the Sea of Galilee called the Twelve, wrought miracles, and spoke words of wisdom and peace, which in due season hung on the Cross, lay in the tomb, rose from the dead, and now reigns in heaven.

I praise, and bless, and give myself wholly to him, who is the true Bread of my soul and my everlasting joy.

1

Hope in God the Creator

God has created all things for good, all things for their greatest good, everything for its own good. What is the good of one is not the good of another; what makes one man happy would make another unhappy. God has determined, unless I interfere with his plan, that I should reach that which will be my greatest happiness. He looks on me individually, he calls me by my name, he knows what I can do, what I can best be, what is my greatest happiness, and he means to give it to me.

God knows what is my greatest happiness, but I do not. There is no rule about what is happy and good; what suits one would not suit another. And the ways by which perfection is reached vary very much; the medicines necessary for our souls are very different from each other. Thus God leads us by strange ways. We know he wills our happiness, but we neither know what our happiness is, nor the way. We are blind. Left to ourselves we would take the wrong way; we must leave it to him. Let us put ourselves into his hands and not be startled even though he leads us by a strange way, a *mirabilis via*, as the Church speaks. Let us be sure he will lead us right, that he will bring us to that which is, not indeed what we think best, nor what is best for another, but what is best for us.

O my God, I will put myself without reserve into your hands. Wealth or woe, joy or sorrow, friends or bereavement, honor or humiliation, good report or ill report, comfort or discomfort, your presence or the hiding of your countenance: all is good if it comes from you. You are wisdom and love—what can I desire more? You have led me in your counsel, and with glory have you received me. What have I in heaven, and apart from you what want I upon earth? My flesh and my heart fail: but God is the God of my heart, and my portion forever.

God was all complete, all blessed in himself, but it was his will to create a world for his glory. He is almighty and might have done all things himself, but it has been his will to bring about his purposes by the beings he has created. We are all created to his glory; we are created to do his will.

I am created to do something or to be something for which no one else is created. I have a place in God's counsels, in God's world, which no one else has. Whether I be rich or poor, despised or esteemed by man, God knows me and calls me by my name.

God has created me to do him some definite service; he has committed some work to me which he has not committed to another. I have my mission — I may never know it in this life, but I shall be told it in the next. Somehow I am necessary for his purposes, as necessary in my place as an archangel in his — if, indeed, I fail, God can raise another, as he could make the stones children of Abraham. Yet I have a part in this great work; I am a link in a chain, a bond of connection between persons. He has not created me for naught.

I shall do good. I shall do his work. I shall be an angel of peace, a preacher of truth in my own place, though not intending it, if I do but keep his commandments and serve him in my calling.

Therefore I will trust him. Whatever, wherever I am, I can never be thrown away. If I am in sickness, my sickness may serve him; in perplexity, my perplexity may serve him; if I am in sorrow, my sorrow may serve him. My sickness, or perplexity, or sorrow may be necessary causes of some great end, which is quite beyond us. He does nothing in vain. He may prolong my life; he may shorten it. He knows what he is about. He may take away my friends. He may throw me among strangers. He may make me feel desolate, make my spirits sink, hide the future from me—still he knows what he is about.

O Adonai, O Ruler of Israel, you who guide Joseph like a flock, O Emmanuel, O Sapientia, I give myself to you. I trust you wholly. You are wiser than I—more loving to me than I am to myself. Deign to fulfill your high purposes in me whatever they be—work in and through me. I am born to serve you, to be yours, to be your instrument. Let me be your blind instrument. I ask not to see. I ask not to know. I ask simply to be used.

2

Hope Inspired by God's Love

What mind of man can imagine the love which the eternal Father bears toward the only-begotten Son? It has been from everlasting, and it is infinite. So great is it that divines call the Holy Spirit by the name of that love, as if to express its infinitude and perfection. Yet reflect, O my soul, and bow down before the awesome mystery, that, as the Father loves the Son, so does the Son love you, if you are one of his elect, for he says expressly, "As the Father has loved me, I also have loved you. Abide in my love" (John 15:9). What mystery in the whole circle of revealed truths is greater than this?

The love which the Son bears toward you, a creature, is like that which the Father bears toward the uncreated Son. O wonderful mystery! *This*, then, is the history of what else is so strange: that he should have taken my flesh and died for me. The former mystery anticipates the latter; the latter does but fulfill the former. If he did not love me so inexpressibly, he would not have suffered for me. I understand now why he died for me, because he loved me as a father loves his son — not as a human father merely, but as the eternal Father loves the eternal Son. I see now the meaning of that otherwise inexplicable humiliation: he preferred to regain me rather than to create new worlds.

How constant is he in his affection! He has loved us from the time of Adam. He has said from the beginning, "I will never leave you nor forsake you" (Deut. 31:6). He did not forsake us in our sin. He did not forsake me. He found me out and regained me. He made a point of it; he resolved to restore me, in spite of myself, to that blessedness which I was so obstinately set against. And now what does he ask of me but that, as he has loved me with an everlasting love, so I should love him in such poor measures as I can show. O mystery of mysteries, that the ineffable love of the Father toward the Son should be the love of the Son toward us! Why was it, O Lord? What good thing did you see in me, a sinner? Why were you set on me? "What is man, that thou are mindful of him, and the son of man that thou should visit him" (Ps. 8:4)? This poor flesh of mine, this weak, sinful soul, which has no life except in your grace, you set your love upon. Complete your work, O Lord, and as you have loved me from the beginning, so make me to love you unto the end.

3

The Mental Sufferings of Our Lord

After all his discourses were consummated (Matt. 26), fully finished, and brought to an end, he said: The Son of Man will be betrayed to crucifixion. As an army puts itself in battle array, as sailors, before an action, clear the decks, as dying men make their will and then turn to God, so, though our Lord could never cease to speak good words, did he sum up and complete his teaching and then commence his Passion. Then he removed by his own act the prohibition that kept Satan from him and opened the door to the agitations of his human heart, as a soldier, who is to suffer death, may drop his handkerchief himself. At once Satan came on and seized upon his brief hour.

An evil temper of murmuring and criticism is spread among the disciples. One was the source of it, but it seems to have been spread. The thought of his death was before him, and he was thinking of it and his burial after it. A woman came and anointed his sacred head. The action spread a soothing tender feeling over his pure soul. It was a mute token of sympathy, and the whole house was filled with it. It was rudely broken by the harsh voice of the traitor, now for the first time giving utterance to his secret heartlessness and malice: *Ut quid perditio haec?* "To what purpose is this waste?" (Matt. 26:8) — the unjust steward with his impious economy making up for his own private thefts by grudging honor to his Master. Thus in the midst of the sweet calm harmony of that feast at Bethany, there comes a jar and discord; all is wrong: sour discontent and distrust are spreading, for the Devil is abroad.

Judas, having once shown what he was, lost no time in carrying out his malice. He went to the chief priests and bargained with them to betray his Lord for a price. Our Lord saw all that took place within him. He saw Satan knocking at his heart, and admitted there, and made an honored and beloved guest and an intimate. He saw him go to the priests and heard the conversation between them. He had seen it by his foreknowledge all the time Judas had been about him and when he chose him. What we know feebly about something to happen affects us far more vividly and very differently when it actually takes place. Our Lord had at length felt, and suffered himself to feel, the cruelty of the ingratitude of which he was the sport and victim. He had treated Judas as one of his most familiar friends. He had shown marks of the closest intimacy; he had made him the purse-keeper of himself and his followers. He had given him the power of working miracles. He had admitted him to a knowledge of the mysteries of the kingdom of heaven. He had sent him out to preach and made him one of his own special representatives, so that the Master was judged by the conduct of his servant.

A heathen, when smitten by a friend, said, "*Et tu, Brute!*" What desolation is in the sense of ingratitude! God, who is met with ingratitude daily, cannot by his nature feel it. He took a human heart, so that he might feel it in its fullness. And now, O my God, though in heaven, do you not feel my ingratitude toward you?

4

Behold the Man

I see the figure of a man, whether young or old I cannot tell. He may be fifty, or he may be thirty. Sometimes he looks one, sometimes the other. There is something inexpressible about his face that I cannot solve. Perhaps, as he bears *all* burdens, he bears that of old age too. But so it is; his face is at once most venerable, yet most childlike, most calm, most sweet, most modest, beaming with sanctity and with loving kindness. His eyes rivet me and move my heart. His breath is all fragrant and transports me out of myself. Oh, I will look upon that face forever and will not cease.

And I see suddenly someone come to him and raise his hand and sharply strike him on that heavenly face. It is a hard hand, the hand of a rude man, and perhaps has iron upon it. It could not be so sudden as to take by surprise him who knows all things past and future, and he shows no sign of resentment, remaining calm and grave as before; but the expression of his face is marred; a great welt arises, and in a short time that all-gracious face is hidden from me by the effects of this indignity, as if a cloud came over it.

A hand was lifted up against the face of Christ. Whose hand was that? My conscience tells me: "You are the man." I trust it is not so with me now. But, O my soul, contemplate the awful fact. *Fancy* Christ before you, and *fancy* yourself lifting up your hand and striking him! You will say, "It is impossible: I could not do so." Yes, you have done so. When you sinned willfully, then you have done so. He is beyond pain now: still you have struck him, and had it been in the days of his flesh, he would have felt pain. Turn back in memory, and recollect the time, the day, the hour, when by willful mortal sin, by scoffing at sacred things, or by profaneness, or by dark hatred of your brother, or by acts of impurity, or by deliberate rejection of God's voice, or in any other devilish way known to you, you have struck the All-Holy One.

O injured Lord, what can I say? I am very guilty concerning you, my brother; and I shall sink in sullen despair if you do not raise me. I cannot look on you; I shrink from you; I throw my arms round my face; I crouch to the earth. Satan will pull me down if you take not pity. It is terrible to turn to you; but oh, turn me, and so shall I be turned. It is a purgatory to endure the sight of you, the sight of myself—I most vile, you most holy. Yet make me look once more on you whom I have so incomprehensibly affronted, for your countenance is my only life, my only hope and health lies in looking on you whom I have pierced. So I put myself before you; I look on you again; I endure the pain in order to receive the purification.

O my God, how can I look you in the face when I think of my ingratitude, so deeply seated, so habitual, so immovable—or rather so awfully increasing! You load me day by day with your favors and feed me with yourself, as you did Judas, yet not only do I not profit thereby, but I do not even make any acknowledgment at the time. Lord, how long? When shall I be free from this real, this fatal captivity? He who made Judas his prey has got foothold of me in my old age, and I cannot get loose. It is the same day after day. When will you give me a still greater grace than you have given, the grace to profit by the graces that you give? When will you give me your effectual grace, which alone can give life and vigor to this effete, miserable, dying soul of mine? My God, I know not in what sense I can pain you in your glorified state; but I know that every fresh sin, every fresh ingratitude I now commit, was among the blows and stripes that once fell on you in your Passion. Oh, let me have as little share in those your past sufferings as possible. Day by day goes, and I find I have been more and more, by the new sins of each day, the cause of them. I know that at best I have a real share of them all, but still it is shocking to find myself having a greater and greater share. Let others wound you—let not me. Let me not have to think that you would have had this or that pang of soul or body the less, except for me. O my God, I am so fast in prison that I cannot get out. O Mary, pray for me.

5

Our Lord Refuses Sympathy

Sympathy may be called an eternal law, for it is signified or rather transcendentally and archetypically fulfilled in the ineffable mutual love of the Divine Trinity. God, though infinitely one, has ever been three. He has ever rejoiced in his Son and his Spirit, and they in him — and thus through all eternity he has existed, not solitary, even though alone, having in this incomprehensible multiplication of himself and reiteration of his person such infinitely perfect bliss that nothing he has created can add anything to it. The Devil only is barren and lonely, shut up in himself — and his servants also.

When, for our sakes, the Son came on earth and took our flesh, he would not live without the sympathy of others. For thirty years he lived with Mary and Joseph and thus formed a shadow of the heavenly Trinity on earth. Oh, the perfection of that sympathy that existed between the three! Not a single look of one was not understood, as

expressed, better than if expressed in a thousand words —
nay, more than understood: accepted, echoed, corrobo-
rated—by the other two. It was like three instruments
absolutely in tune that all vibrate when one vibrates,
and vibrate either one and the same note, or in perfect
harmony.

The first weakening of that unison was when Joseph
died. It was no jar in the sound, for to the last moment of
his life, he was one with them, and the sympathy between
the three only became more intense, and more sweet,
while it was brought into new circumstances and had a
wider range in the months of his declining, his sickness,
and his death. Then it was like an air ranging through
a number of notes performed perfectly and exactly in
time and tune by all three. But it ended in a lower note
than before and, when Joseph went, a weaker one. Not
that Joseph, though so saintly, added much in volume of
sound to the other two, but sympathy, by its very meaning, implies number, and on his death, one out of three
harps was unstrung and silent.

Oh, what a moment of sympathy between the three,
the moment before Joseph died—they supporting and
hanging over him, he looking at them and reposing in
them with undivided, unreserved, supreme devotion, for
he was in the arms of God and the Mother of God. As

a flame shoots up and expires, so was the ecstasy of that last moment ineffable, for each knew and thought of the reverse that was to follow on the snapping of that bond. One moment, very different, of joy, not of sorrow, was equal to it in intensity of feeling: that of the birth of Jesus. The birth of Jesus, the death of Joseph, moments of unutterable sweetness, unparalleled in the history of mankind. St. Joseph went to limbo, to wait his time out of God's presence. Jesus had to preach, suffer, and die; Mary to witness his sufferings and, even after he had risen again, to go on living without him amid the changes of life and the heartlessness of the heathen.

The birth of Jesus, the death of Joseph: those moments of transcendentally pure and perfect and living sympathy between the three members of this earthly trinity, were its beginning and its end. The death of Joseph, which broke it up, was the breaking up of more than itself. It was but the beginning of that change which was coming over Son and Mother. Going on now for thirty years, each of them had been preserved from the world and had lived for each other. Now he had to go out to preach and suffer, and, as the foremost and most inevitable of his trials, and one that from first to last he voluntarily undertook, even when not imperative, he deprived himself of the enjoyment of that intercommunion of hearts — of his heart with the heart of Mary—which had been his from the time he took man's nature, and which he had possessed in an archetypal and transcendent manner with his Father and his Spirit from all eternity.

O my soul, you are allowed to contemplate this union of the three, and to share its sympathy, by faith though not by sight. My God, I believe and know that then a communion of heavenly things was opened on earth that has never been suspended. It is my duty and my bliss to enter into it myself. It is my duty and my bliss to be in tune with that most touching music which then began to sound. Give me that grace which alone can make me hear and understand it, that it may thrill through me. Let the breathings of my soul be with Jesus, Mary, and Joseph. Let me live in obscurity, out of the world and the world's thought, with them. Let me look to them in sorrow and in joy, and live and die in their sweet sympathy.

6

The Priesthood of Jesus

The last day of the earthly exchange between Jesus and Mary was at the marriage feast at Cana. Yet even then there was something taken from that blissful intimacy, for they no longer lived simply for each other, but showed themselves in public and began to take their place in the dispensation that was opening. He manifested forth his glory by his first miracle; and hers also, by making her intercession the medium of it. He honored her still more by breaking through the appointed order of things for her sake and, though his time of miracles had not come, anticipating it at her request. While he wrought his miracle, however, he took leave of her in the words, "Woman, what is between you and me?" Thus he parted with her absolutely, though he parted with a blessing. It was leaving paradise feeble and alone.

For in truth it was fitting that he who was to be the true High Priest, should thus, while he exercised his office for the whole race of man, be free from all human ties and sympathies of the flesh. And one reason for his long abode at Nazareth with his Mother may have been to show that, as he gave up his Father's and his own glory on high to become man, so he gave up the innocent and pure joys of his earthly home to be a priest. So, in the old time, Melchizedek is described as without father or mother (Heb. 7:3). So the Levites showed themselves truly worthy of the sacerdotal office and were made the sacerdotal tribe, because they steeled themselves against natural affection, said to father or mother, "I know you not," and raised the sword against their own kindred, when the honor of the Lord of armies demanded the sacrifice.

In like manner our Lord said to Mary, "What is between me and you?" It was the setting apart of the sacrifice, the first ritual step of the great act that was to be solemnly performed for the salvation of the world. "What is between me and you, O woman?" is the offertory before the oblation of the Host. O my dear Lord, you who have given up your mother for me, give me grace cheerfully to give up all my earthly friends and relations for you.

The great High Priest said to his kindred, "I know you not." Then, as he did so, we may believe that the most tender heart of Jesus looked back upon his whole time since his birth and called before him those former days of his infancy and childhood, when he had been with others from whom he had long been parted. Time was when St. Elizabeth and the Holy Baptist had formed part of the Holy Family. St. Elizabeth, like St. Joseph, had been removed by death and was waiting his coming to break that bond that detained both her and St. Joseph from heaven. St. John had been cut off from his home and mankind and the sympathies of earth, long since, and had now begun to preach the coming Savior and was waiting and expecting his manifestation.

Give me grace, O Jesus, to live in sight of that blessed company. Let my life be spent in the presence of you and your dearest friends. Even though I see them not, let not what I do see seduce me to give my heart elsewhere. Because you have blessed me so much and given to me friends, let me not depend or rely or throw myself in any way upon them, but in you be my life and my conversation and daily walk among those with whom you surrounded yourself on earth and who now delight you in heaven. Be my soul with you and, because with you, with Mary and Joseph and Elizabeth and John.

Nor did Jesus, as time went on, give up Mary and Joseph only. There still remained to him invisible attendants and friends, and he had their sympathy, but them also he at length gave up. From the time of his birth we may suppose he held communion with the spirits of the old fathers, who had prepared his coming and prophesied of it. On one occasion he was seen conversing with Moses and Elijah, and that conversation was about his Passion.

What a field of thought is thus opened to us, of which we know how little. When he passed whole nights in prayer, it was greater refreshment to soul and body than sleep. Who could support and (so to say) reinvigorate the divine Lord better than that praiseworthy company of prophets of which he was the fulfillment? Then he might talk with Abraham, who saw his day (cf. John 8:56), or with Moses, who spoke to him; or with his especial types, David and Jeremiah; or with those who spoke most of him, as Isaiah and Daniel. And here was a fund of great sympathy. When he came up to Jerusalem to suffer, he might be met in spirit by all the holy priests who had offered sacrifices in shadow of him; just as now the priest recalls in Mass the sacrifices of Abel, Abraham, and Melchizedek, and the fiery gift that purged the lips of Isaiah (cf. Isa. 6:7), as well as holding communion with the Apostles and martyrs.

7

The Sorrows of Mary

Let us linger for a while with Mary — before we follow the steps of her Son, our Lord. There was an occasion when he refused to let someone bid his own home farewell before following him (Luke 9:59–60); and such was, as it seems, almost his own way with his mother; but will he be displeased if we for one instant stop with her, even though our meditation lies with him?

O Mary, we are devout to your seven woes. But was not this, though not one of those seven, one of the greatest, and included those that followed, from your knowledge of them beforehand? How did you bear that first separation from him? How did the first days pass when you were desolate? Where did you hide yourself? Where did you pass the long three years and more, while he was on his ministry? Once — at the beginning of it — you did attempt to get near him, and then we hear nothing of you, until we find you standing at his Cross.

The Sorrows of Mary

And then, after that great joy of seeing him again, and the permanent consolation, never to be lost, that with him all suffering and humiliation was over, and that never had she to weep for him again, still she was separated from him for many years, while she lived in the flesh, surrounded by the wicked world, and in the misery of his absence.

The blessed Mary, among her other sorrows, suffered the loss of her Son after he had lived under the same roof with her for thirty years. When he was no more than twelve, he gave her a token of what was to be and said, "I must be about my Father's business" (Luke 2:49); and when the time came and he began his miracles, he said to her, "What is to me and to you?" (John 2:4)—What is common to us two?—and soon he left her. Once she tried to see him, but in vain; and then at the last, once more she tried, and she reached him in time to see him hanging on the Cross and dying. He was only forty days on earth after his Resurrection, and then he left her in old age to finish her life without him. Compare her thirty happy years and her time of desolation.

I see her in her forlorn home, while her Son and Lord was going up and down the land without a place to lay his head, suffering both because she was so desolate and he was so exposed. How dreary passed the day; and then came reports that he was in some peril or distress. She heard, perhaps, he had been led into the wilderness to be tempted. She would have shared all his sufferings, but was not permitted. Once there was a profane report, which was believed by many, that he was beside himself, and his friends and kindred went out to get possession of him. She went out too to see him and tried to reach him. She could not for the crowd. A message came to him to that effect, but he made no effort to receive her, nor said a kind word. She went back to her home disappointed, without the sight of him. And so she remained, perhaps in company with those who did not believe in him.

I see her too after his Ascension. This too is a time of bereavement, but still of consolation. It was still a twilight time, but not a time of grief. The Lord was absent, but he was not on earth; he was not in suffering. Death had no power over him. And he came to her day by day in the Blessed Sacrifice. I see the Blessed Mary at Mass, and St. John celebrating. She is waiting for the moment of her Son's presence: now she converses with him in the sacred rite; and what shall I say now? She receives him, to whom once she gave birth.

O Holy Mother, stand by me now at Mass time, when Christ comes to me, as you ministered to your infant Lord, as you hung upon his words when he grew up, as you were found under his Cross. Stand by me, Holy Mother, that I may gain somewhat of your purity, your innocence, your faith, and he may be the one object of my love and my adoration, as he was of yours.

8

The Bodily Sufferings of Our Lord

Our Lord's bodily pains were greater than those of any martyr because he willed them to be greater. All pain of body depends—as to be felt at all, so to be felt in this or that degree—on the nature of the living mind that dwells in that body. Vegetables have no feeling because they have no living mind or spirit within them. Brute animals feel more or less according to the intelligence within them. Man feels more than any brute, because he has a soul. Christ's soul felt more than that of any other man, because his soul was exalted by personal union with the Word of God. Christ felt bodily pain more keenly than any other man, as much as man feels pain more keenly than any other animal.

It is a relief to pain to have the thoughts drawn another way. Thus, soldiers in battle often do not know when they are wounded. Again, persons in raging fevers seem to suffer a great deal; then afterward they can but recollect general discomfort and restlessness. And so excitement and enthusiasm are great alleviations of bodily pain; thus savages die at the stake amid torments singing songs; it is a sort of mental drunkenness. And so again, an instantaneous pain is comparatively bearable; it is the continuance of pain which is so heavy, and if we had no memory of the pain we suffered last minute, and also suffer in the present, we would find pain easy to bear; but what makes the second pang grievous is that there has been a first pang; and what makes the third more grievous is that there has been a first and a second; the pain seems to grow because it is prolonged.

Now Christ suffered, not as in a delirium or in excitement, or in inadvertency, but he looked pain in the face! He offered his whole mind to it and received it, as it were, directly into his bosom and suffered all he suffered with a full consciousness of suffering.

Christ would not drink the drugged cup that was offered to him to cloud his mind (cf. Matt. 27:34). He willed to have the full sense of pain. His soul was so intently fixed on his suffering as not to be distracted from it; and it was so active, and recollected the past and anticipated the future, and the whole Passion was, as it were, concentrated on each moment of it, and all that he had suffered and all that he was to suffer lent its aid to increase what he was suffering. Yet withal his soul was so calm and sober and unexcited as to be passive and thus to receive the full burden of the pain on it, without the power of throwing it off him. Moreover, the sense of conscious innocence, and the knowledge that his sufferings would come to an end, might have supported him; but he repressed the comfort and turned away his thoughts from these alleviations so that he might suffer absolutely and perfectly.

O my God and Savior, who went through such sufferings for me with such lively consciousness, such precision, such recollection, and such fortitude, enable me, by your help, if I am brought into the power of this terrible trial, bodily pain, enable me to bear it with some portion of your calmness. Obtain for me this grace, O Virgin Mother, who saw your Son suffer and suffered with him; that I, when I suffer, may associate my sufferings with his and with yours, and that through his Passion, and your merits, and those of all saints, they may be a satisfaction for my sins and procure for me eternal life.

9

The Passion of Our Lord

Our Lord's sufferings were so great because his soul was in suffering. What shows this is that his soul began to suffer before his bodily passion, as we see in the agony in the garden.

The first anguish that came upon his body was not from without—it was not from the scourges, the thorns, or the nails, but from his soul. His soul was in such agony that he called it death: "My soul is sorrowful even unto death" (Mark 14:34). The anguish was such that it burst open his whole body, as it were. It was a pang affecting his heart, as, in the deluge, the floods of the great deep were broken up and the windows of heaven were opened. The blood, rushing from his tormented heart, forced its way on every side, formed for itself a thousand new channels, filled all the pores, and at length stood forth upon his skin in thick drops, which fell heavily on the ground (cf. Luke 22:44).

He remained in this living death from the time of his agony in the garden; and as his first agony was from his soul, so was his last. As the scourge and the Cross did not begin his sufferings, so they did not close them. It was the agony of his soul, not of his body, which caused his death. His persecutors were surprised to hear that he was dead. How, then, did he die? That agonized, tormented heart, which at the beginning so awfully relieved itself in the rush of blood and the bursting of his pores, at length broke. It broke, and he died. It would have broken *at once,* had he not kept it from breaking. At length the moment came. He gave the word, and his heart broke.

O tormented heart, it was love and sorrow and fear that broke you. It was the sight of human sin, it was the sense of it, the feeling of it laid on you; it was zeal for the glory of God, horror at seeing sin so near you, a sickening, stifling feeling at its pollution, the deep shame and disgust and abhorrence and revolt it inspired, keen pity for the souls whom it has drawn headlong into hell—all these feelings together you allowed to rush upon you. You submitted yourself to their powers, and they were your death. That strong heart; that all-noble, all-generous, all-tender, all-pure heart was slain by sin.

O most tender and gentle Lord Jesus, when will my heart have a portion of your perfections? When will my hard and stony heart, my proud heart, my unbelieving heart, my impure heart, my narrow, selfish heart be melted and conformed to yours? Oh, teach me so to contemplate you that I may become like you and to love you sincerely and simply, as you have loved me.

It is over now, O Lord, as with your sufferings, so with our humiliations. We have followed you from your fasting in the wilderness till your death on the Cross. For forty days we have professed to do penance. The time has been long, and it has been short; but whether long or short, it is now over. It is over, and we feel a pleasure that it is over; it is a relief and a release. We thank you that it is over. We thank you for the time of sorrow, but we thank you more as we look forward to the time of festival. Pardon our shortcomings in Lent and reward us in Easter.

We have, indeed, done very little for you, O Lord. We recollect well our listlessness and weariness; our indisposition to mortify ourselves when we had no plea of health to stand in the way; our indisposition to pray and to meditate, our disorder of mind, our discontent, our peevishness. Yet some of us, perhaps, have done something for you. Look on us as a whole, O Lord, look on us as a community, and let what some have done well plead for us all.

O Lord, the end is come. We are conscious of our languor and lukewarmness; we do not deserve to rejoice in Easter, yet we cannot help doing so. We feel more of pleasure, we rejoice in you more than our past humiliation warrants us in doing; yet may that very joy be its own warrant. Oh, be indulgent to us, for the merits of your own all-powerful Passion, and for the merits of your saints. Accept us as your little flock, in the day of small things, in a fallen country, in an age when faith and love are scarce. Pity us and spare us and give us peace.

O my own Savior, now in the tomb but soon to arise, you have paid the price; it is done — *consummatum est* — it is secured. Oh, fulfill your Resurrection in us, and as you have purchased us, claim us, take possession of us, make us yours.

10

God, the Blessedness of the Soul

To possess you, O Lover of Souls, is happiness, and the only happiness of the immortal soul! To enjoy the sight of you is the only happiness of eternity. At present I might amuse and sustain myself with the vanities of sense and time, but they will not last forever. We shall be stripped of them when we pass out of this world. All shadows will one day be gone. And what shall I do then? There will be nothing left to me but the almighty God. If I cannot take pleasure in the thought of him, there is no one else then to take pleasure in; God and my soul will be the only two beings left in the whole world, as far as I am concerned. He will be all in all, whether I wish it or not. What a strait I shall then be in if I do not love him, and there is then nothing else to love; if I feel averse to him, and he is then ever looking upon me!

Ah, my dear Lord, how can I bear to say that you will be all in all, whether I wish it or not? Should I not wish it with my whole heart? What can give me happiness but you? If I had all the resources of time and sense about me, just as I have now, should I not in course of ages, nay of years, weary of them? If this world were to last forever, would it be able ever to supply my soul with food? Is there any earthly thing that I do not weary of at length even now? Do old men love what young men love? Is there not constant change?

I am sure then, my God, that the time would come, though it might be long in coming, when I would have exhausted all the enjoyment the world could give. You alone, my dear Lord, are the food for eternity, and you alone. You only can satisfy the soul of man. Eternity would be misery without you, even though you did not inflict punishment. To see you, to gaze on you, to contemplate you: this alone is inexhaustible. You indeed are unchangeable, yet in you there are always more glorious depths and more varied attributes to search into; we shall ever be beginning as if we had never gazed upon you. In your presence are torrents of delight, and whoever tastes them will never let go. This is my true portion, O my Lord, here and hereafter!

My God, how far am I from acting according to what I know so well! I confess it: my heart goes after shadows. I love anything better than communion with you. I am ever eager to get away from you. Often I find it difficult even to say my prayers. There is hardly any amusement I would not rather take up than set myself to think of you. Give me, grace, O my Father, to be utterly ashamed of my own reluctance! Rouse me from sloth and coldness, and make me desire you with my whole heart. Teach me to love meditation, sacred reading, and prayer. Teach me to love that which must engage my mind for all eternity.

11

Jesus Christ, Yesterday, and Today, and the Same Forever

All things change here below. I say it, O Lord; I believe it; and I shall feel it more and more the longer I live. Before your eyes, most awesome Lord, the whole future of my life lies bare. You know exactly what will befall me every year and every day until my last hour. And though I know not what you see concerning me, so much I know: that you read in my life perpetual change. Not a year will leave me as it found me, either within or without. I never shall remain any time in one state. How many things are sure to happen to me, unexpected, sudden, hard to bear! I know them not. I know not how long I have to live. I am hurried on, whether I will it or not, through continual change. O my God, in what can I trust? There is nothing in which I dare trust; nay, if I trusted in anything of earth, I believe for that very reason it would be taken away from me. I know you would take it away, if you had love for me.

Jesus Christ, Yesterday, and Today

Everything short of you, O Lord, is changeable, but you endure. You are ever one and the same — ever the true God of man and unchangeably so. You are the rarest, most precious, the sole good; and withal you are the most lasting. The creature changes, the Creator never. The creature stops changing only when it rests in you. On you the angels look and are at peace; that is why they have perfect bliss. They never can lose their blessedness, for they never can lose you. They have no anxiety, no misgivings because they love the Creator; not any being of time and sense, but "Jesus Christ, the same yesterday and today, who is also for ever" (Heb. 13:8).

My Lord, my only God, *Deus meus et omnia*, let me never go after vanities. *Vanitas vanitatum et omnia vanitas* (Eccles. 1:2). All is vanity and shadow here below. Let me not give my heart to anything here. Let nothing allure me from you; oh, keep me wholly and entirely. Keep this most frail heart and this most weak head in your divine keeping. Draw me to you morning, noon, and night for consolation. Be my own bright light, to which I look, for guidance and for peace. Let me love you, O my Lord Jesus, with a pure affection and a fervent affection! Let me love you with the fervor, only greater, with which men of this earth love beings of this earth. Let me have that tenderness and constancy in loving you which is so much praised among men, when the object is of the earth. Let me find and feel you to be my only joy, my only refuge, my only strength, my only comfort, my only hope, my only fear, my only love.

12

An Act of Love

You are the Supreme Good. And, in saying so, I mean not only supreme goodness and benevolence, but that you are the sovereign and transcendent beautifulness. I believe that, beautiful as is your creation, it is mere dust and ashes, and of no account, compared with you, who are the infinitely more beautiful Creator. I know well therefore that the angels and saints have such perfect bliss because they see you. To see even the glimpse of your true glory, even in this world, throws holy men into an ecstasy. And I feel the truth of all this, in my own degree, because you have mercifully taken our nature upon you and have come to me as man. *Et vidimus gloriam ejus, gloriam quasi Unigeniti a Patre* — "And we saw His glory, the glory as it were of the only begotten of the Father" (John 1:14). The more, O my dear Lord, I meditate on your words, works, actions, and sufferings in the Gospel, the more wonderfully glorious and beautiful I see you to be.

And therefore, O my dear Lord, since I perceive you to be so beautiful, I love you and desire to love you more and more. Since you are the one Goodness, Beautifulness, Gloriousness in the whole world of being, and there is nothing like you, but you are infinitely more glorious and good than even the most beautiful of creatures, therefore I love you with a singular love, a one, only, sovereign love. Everything, O my Lord, shall be dull and dim to me, after looking at you. There is nothing on earth, not even what is most naturally dear to me, that I can love in comparison with you. And I would lose everything whatever rather than lose you. For you, O my Lord, are my supreme and only Lord and love.

My God, you know infinitely better than I how little I love you. I would not love you at all except for your grace. It is your grace that has opened the eyes of my mind and enabled them to see your glory. It is your grace that has touched my heart and brought upon it the influence of what is so wonderfully beautiful and fair. How can I help loving you, O my Lord, except by some dreadful perversion, which hinders me from looking at you? O my God, whatever is nearer to me than you, things of this earth, and things more naturally pleasing to me, will be sure to interrupt the sight of you, unless your grace interferes. Keep my eyes, my ears, my heart from any such miserable tyranny. Break my bonds — raise my heart. Keep my whole being fixed on you. Let me never lose sight of you; and, while I gaze on you, let my love of you grow more and more every day.

13

Against You Only Have I Sinned

You, O Lord, after living a whole eternity in ineffable bliss, because you are the one and sole perfection, at length did begin to create spirits to be with you and to share your blessedness according to their degree; and the return they made you was at once to rebel against you. First a great part of the angels, then mankind have risen up against you and served others, not you. Why did you create us, but to make us happy? Could you be made more happy by creating us? And how could we be happy but in obeying you? Yet we determined not to be happy as you would have us happy, but to find out a happiness of our own; and so we left you.

O my God, what a return is it that we — that I — make you when we sin! What dreadful unthankfulness is it! And what will be my punishment for refusing to be happy and for preferring hell to heaven! I know what the punishment will be. You will say, "Let him have it all his own way. He wishes to perish; let him perish. He despises the graces I give him; they shall turn to a curse."

You, O my God, have a claim on me, and I am wholly yours! You are the almighty Creator, and I am your workmanship. I am the work of your hands, and you are my owner. As well might the axe or the hammer exalt itself against its framer, as I against you. You owe me nothing. I have no rights in respect to you; I have only duties. I depend on you for life, and health, and every blessing every moment. I have no more power of exercising will as to my life than axe or hammer. I depend on you far more entirely than anything here depends on its owner and master. The son does not depend on the father for the continuance of life — the matter out of which the axe is made existed first — but I depend wholly on you. If you withdraw your breath from me for a moment, I die. I am wholly and entirely your property and your work, and my one duty is to serve you.

O my God, I confess that before now I have utterly forgotten this and that I am continually forgetting it! I have acted many a time as if I were my own master and turned from you rebelliously. I have acted according to my own pleasure, not according to yours. And so far have I hardened myself, as not to feel as I ought how evil this is. I do not understand how dreadful sin is — and I do not hate it and fear it as I ought. I have no horror of it or loathing. I do not turn from it with indignation, as being an insult to you, but I trifle with it, and, even if I do not commit great sins, I have no great reluctance to do small ones. O my God, what a great and awful difference is there between what I am and what I ought to be.

My God, I dare not offend any earthly superior; I am afraid—for I know I shall get into trouble—yet I dare offend you. I know, O Lord, that, according to the greatness of the person offended against, the greater is the offense. Yet I do not fear to offend you, whom to offend is to offend the infinite God. O my dear Lord, how would I myself feel, what would I say of myself, if I were to strike some revered superior on earth? If I were violently to deal a blow upon someone as revered as a father or a priest? If I were to strike him on the face? I cannot bear even to think of such a thing—yet what is this compared with lifting up my hand against you? And what is sin but this? To sin is to insult you in the grossest of all conceivable ways.

This then, O my soul, is what the sinfulness of sin consists in. It is lifting up my hand against my infinite Benefactor, against my almighty Creator, Preserver, and Judge, against him in whom all majesty and glory and beauty and reverence and sanctity center, against the one only God.

Against You Only Have I Sinned

O my God, I am utterly confounded to think of the state in which I lie! What will become of me if you are severe? What is my life, O my dear and merciful Lord, but a series of offenses, little or great, against you! Oh, what great sins I have committed against you before now — and how continually in lesser matters I am sinning!

My God, what will become of me? What will be my position hereafter if I am left to myself! What can I do but come humbly to him whom I have so heavily affronted and insulted and beg him to forgive the debt which lies against me? O my Lord Jesus, whose love for me has been so great as to bring you down from heaven to save me, teach me, dear Lord, my sin. Teach me its heinousness. Teach me truly to repent of it — and pardon it in your great mercy!

I beg you, O my dear Savior, to recover me! Your grace alone can do it. I cannot save myself. I cannot recover my lost ground. I cannot turn to you, I cannot please you, or save my soul without you. I shall go from bad to worse, I shall fall from you entirely, I shall quite harden myself against my neglect of duty, if I rely on my own strength. I shall make myself, intead of you, my center. I shall worship some idol of my own framing instead of you, the only true God and my Maker, unless you hinder it by your grace. O my dear Lord, hear me! I have lived long

enough in this undecided, wavering, unsatisfactory state.
I wish to be your good servant. I wish to sin no more. Be
gracious to me, and enable me to be what I know I ought
to be.

14

The Effects of Sin

My Lord, you are the infinitely merciful God. You love all things that you have created. You are the lover of souls. How then is it, O Lord, that I am in a world so miserable as this is? Can this be the world which you have created, so full of pain and suffering? Who among the sons of Adam lives without suffering from his birth to his death? How many bad sicknesses and diseases are there! How many frightful accidents! How many great anxieties! How are men brought down and broken by grief, distress, the tumult of passions, and continual fear! What dreadful plagues are there ever on the earth: war, famine, and pestilence! Why is this, O my God? Why is this, O my soul? Dwell upon it, and ask yourself: Why is this? Has God changed his nature? Yet how evil has the earth become!

O my God, I know full well why all these evils are. You have not changed your nature, but man has ruined his own. We have sinned, O Lord, and therefore is this change. All these evils that I see and in which I partake are the fruit of sin. They would not have been, had we not sinned. They are but the first installment of the punishment of sin. They are an imperfect and dim image of what sin is. Sin is infinitely worse than famine, than war, than pestilence. Take the most hideous of diseases, under which the body wastes away and corrupts; the blood is infected; the head, the heart, the lungs, every organ disordered; the nerves unstrung and shattered; pain in every limb, thirst, restlessness, delirium—all is nothing compared with that dreadful sickness of the soul which we call sin. They all are the effects of it; they all are shadows of it but nothing more. That cause itself is something different in kind, is of a malignity far other and greater than all these things. O my God, teach me this! Give me to understand the enormity of that evil under which I labor and know it not. Teach me what sin is.

All these dreadful pains of body and soul are the fruits of sin, but they are nothing to its punishment in the world to come. The keenest and fiercest of bodily pains is nothing compared with the fire of hell; the most dire horror or anxiety is nothing compared with the never-dying worm of conscience; the greatest bereavement, loss of substance, desertion of friends, and forlorn desolation is nothing compared with the loss of God's countenance.

The Effects of Sin

Eternal punishment is the only true measure of the guilt of sin. My God, teach me this. Open my eyes and heart, I earnestly pray you, and make me understand how awful a body of death I bear about me. And, not only teach me about it, but in your mercy and by your grace remove it.

15

The Evil of Sin

My God, I know that you created the whole universe very good; and if this was true of the material world that we see, much more true is it of the world of rational beings. The innumerable stars that fill the firmament and the very elements out of which the earth is made: all are carried through their courses and their operations in perfect concord; but much higher was the concord that reigned in heaven when the angels were first created. At that first moment of their existence the main orders of the angels were in the most excellent harmony, and beautiful to contemplate; and the creation of man was expected next to continue that harmony in the instance of a different kind of being.

Then it was that suddenly was discovered a flaw or a rent in one point of this most delicate and exquisite web, and it extended and unraveled the web, until a third part of it was spoiled; and then again a similar flaw was found in humankind, and it extended over the whole race. This dreadful evil, destroying so large a portion of all God's works, is sin.

My God, such is sin in your judgment. What is it in the judgment of the world? A very small evil or none at all. In the judgment of the Creator it is that which has marred his spiritual work; it is a greater evil than if the stars had gotten loose and ran wild in heaven, and chaos came again. But man, who is the guilty one, calls it by soft names. He explains it away. The world laughs at it and is indulgent toward it; and, as to its deserving eternal punishment, the world rises up indignant at the idea, and rather than admit it, would deny the God who has said it does. The world thinks sin the same sort of imperfection as an impropriety, or want of taste, or infirmity. O my soul, consider carefully the great difference between the views of sin taken by almighty God and the world!

Which of the two views do you mean to believe?

O my soul, which of the two will you believe — the word of God or the word of man? Is God right, or is the creature right? Is sin the greatest of all possible evils or the least?

My Lord and Savior, I have no hesitation about which to believe. You are true, and every man a liar. I will believe you above the whole world. My God, imprint on my heart the infamous deformity of sin. Teach me to abhor it as a pestilence; as a fierce flame destroying on every side; as my death. Let me take up arms against it and devote myself to fight under your banner in overcoming it.

16

The Heinousness of Sin

My Lord, I know well that you are all perfect and need nothing. Yet I know that you have taken upon yourself the nature of man, and, not only so, but in that nature came upon earth and suffered all manner of evil and died. This is a history that has hung the heavens with sackcloth and taken from this earth, beautiful as it is, its light and glory. You came, O my dear Lord, and you suffered in no ordinary way, but unheard of and extreme torments! The all-blessed Lord suffered the worst and most various of pains. This is the corner truth of the gospel: it is the one foundation, Jesus Christ and he crucified. I know it, O Lord, I believe it, and I put it steadily before me.

Why is this strange anomaly in the face of nature? Does God do things for naught? No, my soul, it is sin. It is your sin, which has brought the Everlasting down upon earth to suffer. Hence I learn how great an evil sin is. The death of the Infinite is its sole measure. All that slow distress of body and mind which he endured, from the time he shed blood at Gethsemane down to his death, all that pain came from sin. What sort of evil is that, which had to be so encountered by such a sacrifice and to be reversed at such a price! Here then I understand best how horrible a thing sin is. It is horrible, because through it have come upon men all those evils, whatever they are, with which the earth abounds. It is more horrible in that it has nailed the Son of God to the accursed tree.

My dear Lord and Savior, how can I make light of that which has had such consequences! Henceforth I will, through your grace, have deeper views of sin than before. Fools make jest of sin, but I will view things in their true light. My suffering Lord, I have made you suffer. You are most beautiful in your eternal nature, O my Lord. You are most beautiful in your sufferings! Your adorable attributes are not dimmed but are increased to us as we gaze on your humiliation. You are more beautiful to us than before. But still I will never forget that it was man's sin, my sin, which made that humiliation necessary. *Amor meus crucifixus est*—my Love is crucified, but by none other than me. I have crucified you; my sin has crucified you. O my Savior, what a dreadful thought—but I cannot undo it. All I can do is to hate that which made you suffer. Shall I not do that at least? Shall I not love my Lord just so much as to hate that which is so great an enemy of his and to break off all terms with it? Shall I not put off sin altogether? By your great love of me, teach me and enable me to do this, O Lord. Give me a deep, rooted, intense hatred of sin.

17

The Bondage of Sin

You, O my Lord and God, you alone are strong; you alone are holy! You are the *Sanctus Deus, sanctus fortis* — "Holy God, holy and strong!" You are the sanctity and the strength of all things. No created nature has any stay or subsistence in itself but crumbles and melts away, if you are not with it to sustain it. My God, you are the strength of the angels, of the saints in glory, of holy men on earth. No being has any sanctity or any strength apart from you.

My God, I wish to adore you as such. I wish with all my heart to understand and to confess this great truth, that not only are you almighty, but that there is no might at all, or power, or strength, anywhere but in you.

My God, if you are the strength of all spirits, oh, how preeminently are you my strength! Oh, how true it is, so that nothing is more so, that I have no strength but in you! I feel intimately, O my God, that whenever I am left to myself, I go wrong. As sure as a stone falls down to the earth if it is let go, so surely my heart and spirit fall down hopelessly if they are let go by you. You must uphold me by your right hand, or I cannot stand.

How strange it is, but how true, that all my natural tendencies are toward sloth, toward excess, toward neglect of religion, toward neglect of prayer, toward love of the world, not toward love of you, or love of sanctity, or love of self-governance. I approve and praise what I do not do. My heart runs after vanities, and I tend to death; I tend to corruption and dissolution, apart from you, *Deus immortalis*.

My God, I have had experience enough what a dreadful bondage sin is. If you are away, I find I cannot keep myself—however I wish it—and am in the hands of my own self-will, pride, sensuality, and selfishness. And they prevail with me more and more every day, until they are irresistible. In time the old Adam within me gets so strong that I become a mere slave. I confess things to be wrong which nevertheless I do. I bitterly lament over my bondage, but I cannot undo it.

Oh, what a tyranny is sin! It is a heavy weight that cripples me—and what will be the end of it? By your all-precious merits, by your almighty power, I entreat you, O my Lord, to give me life and sanctity and strength!

Deus sanctus, give me holiness; *Deus fortis*, give me strength; *Deus immortalis*, give me perseverance. *Sanctus Deus, Sanctus fortis, Sanctus immortalis, miserere nobis.*

18

Every Sin Has Its Punishment

You are the all-seeing, all-knowing God. Your eyes, O Lord, are in every place. You are a real spectator of everything that takes place anywhere. You are ever with me. You are present and conscious of all I think, say, or do—you, God, who have seen me. Every deed or act, however slight; every word, however quick and casual; every thought of my heart, however secret, however momentary, however forgotten, you see, O Lord. You see and you note down. You have a book; you enter in it every day of my life. I forget; you do not forget. There is stored up the history of all my past years, and so it will be until I die—the leaves will be filled and turned over and the book at length finished. *Quo ibo a Spiritu Tuo*—"Whither shall I go from your spirit?" (Ps. 139:7) I am in your hands, O Lord, absolutely.

My God, how often do I act wrongly, how seldom rightly! How dreary on the whole are the acts of any one

63

day! All my sins, offenses, and negligences, not of one day only, but of all days, are in your book. And every sin, offense, and negligence has a separate definite punishment. That list of penalties increases, silently but surely, every day. As the spendthrift is overwhelmed by a continually greater weight of debt, so am I exposed continually to a greater and greater score of punishments catalogued against me. I *forget* the sins of my childhood, my boyhood, my adolescence, my youth. They are all noted down in that book. *There* is a complete history of all my life; and it will one day be brought up against me. Nothing is lost, all is remembered. O my soul, what have you to go through! What an examination that will be, and what a result! I shall have put upon me the punishment of ten thousand sins—I shall for this purpose be sent to purgatory—how long will it last? When shall I ever get out? Not until I have paid the last farthing. When will this possibly be?

O my dear Lord, have mercy upon me! I trust you have forgiven me my sins—but the punishment remains. In the midst of your love for me, and recognizing me as your own, you will consign me to purgatory. There I shall go through my sins once more, in their punishment. There I shall suffer, but here is the time for a thorough repentance. Here is the time of good works, of obtaining indulgences, of wiping out the debt in every possible way.

Every Sin Has Its Punishment

Your saints, though seeming to be without sin in the eyes of man, really had a vast account — and they settled it by continual trials here. I have neither their merit nor their sufferings. I cannot tell whether I can make such acts of love as will gain me an indulgence of my sins. The prospect before me is dark, and I can only rely on your infinite compassion. O my dear Lord, who have in so many ways shown your mercy toward me, pity me here! Be merciful in the midst of justice.

19

The Power of the Cross

O my God, who could have imagined, by any light of nature, that it was one of your attributes to lower yourself and to work out your purposes by your own humiliation and suffering? You had lived from eternity in ineffable blessedness. My God, I might have understood as much as this: that, when you did begin to create and surround yourself with a world of creatures, that these attributes would show themselves in you which before had no exercise. You could not show your power when there was nothing whatever to exercise it. Then too, you did begin to show your wonderful and tender providence, your faithfulness, your solicitous care for those whom you had created. But who could have fancied that your creation of the universe implied and involved in it your humiliation? O my great God, you have humbled yourself, you have stooped to take our flesh and blood and have been lifted up upon the tree! I praise and glorify you tenfold the more, because you have shown your power by means of your suffering, than had you carried on your work without it. It is worthy of your infinitude thus to surpass and transcend all our thoughts.

O my Lord Jesus, I believe, and by your grace will ever believe and hold, and I know that it is true, and will be true to the end of the world, that nothing great is done without suffering, without humiliation, and that all things are possible by means of it. I believe, O my God, that poverty is better than riches, pain better than pleasure, obscurity and contempt than name, and ignominy and reproach than honor. My Lord, I do not ask you to bring these trials on me, for I know not if I could face them; but at least, O Lord, whether I be in prosperity or adversity, I will believe that it is as I have said. I will never have faith in riches, rank, power, or reputation. I will never set my heart on worldly success or on worldly advantages. I will never wish for what men call the prizes of life. I will ever, with your grace, make much of those who are despised or neglected, honor the poor, revere the suffering, and admire and venerate your saints and confessors and take my part with them in spite of the world.

And lastly, O my dear Lord, though I am so very weak that I am not fit to ask you for suffering as a gift, and have not strength to do so, at least I will beg of you grace to meet suffering well, when you in your love and wisdom bring it upon me. When it comes, let me bear pain, reproach, disappointment, slander, anxiety, suspense as you would have me, O my Jesus, and as you by your own suffering have taught me.

And I promise too, with your grace, that I will never set myself up, never seek preeminence, never court any great thing of the world, never prefer myself to others. I wish to bear insult meekly, and to return good for evil. I wish to humble myself in all things, to be silent when I am ill-used, and to be patient when sorrow or pain is prolonged, and all for the love of you, and your Cross, knowing that in this way I shall gain the promise both of this life and of the next.

20

The Temples of the Holy Spirit

I adore you, O Eternal Word, for your gracious condescension, in taking not only a created nature, a created spirit or soul, but a material body. The Most High decreed that forever and ever he would subject himself to a created prison. He who from eternity was nothing but infinite incomprehensible spirit, beyond all laws but those of his own transcendent greatness, willed that for the eternity to come he should be united, in the most intimate of unions, with that which was under the conditions of a creature.

Your omnipotence, O Lord, ever protects itself—but nothing short of that omnipotence could enable you so to condescend without a loss of power. Your body has part in your power, rather than that you have part in its weakness. For this reason, my God, it was, that you could not but rise again, if you were to die—because your body, once taken by you, never was or could be separated from you, even in the grave. It was your body even then; it could see no corruption; it could not remain under the power of death, for you had already wonderfully made it yours, and whatever was yours must last in its perfection forever. I adore your most holy body, O my dear Jesus, the instrument of our redemption!

I look at you, my Lord Jesus, and think of your most holy body, and I keep it before me as the pledge of my own resurrection. Though I die, as die I certainly shall, nevertheless I shall not forever die, for I shall rise again. My Lord, the heathen who knew you not, thought the body to be of a miserable and contemptible nature — they thought it the seat, the cause, the excuse of all moral evil. When their thoughts soared highest, and they thought of a future life, they considered that the destruction of the body was the condition of that higher existence. That the body was really part of themselves, and that its restoration could be a privilege, was beyond their utmost imagination. And indeed, what mind of man, O Lord, could ever have fancied without your revelation that what, according to our experience, is so vile, so degraded, so animal, so sinful, which is our fellowship with the brutes, which is full of corruption and becomes dust and ashes, was in its very nature capable of so high a destiny — that it could become celestial and immortal, without ceasing to be a body! And who but you, who are omnipotent, could have made it so! No wonder, then, that the wise men of the world, who did not believe in you, scoffed at the Resurrection. But I, by your grace, will ever keep before me how differently I have been taught by you.

O best and first and truest of teachers! O you who are the truth, I know, and believe with my whole heart, that this very flesh of mine will rise again. I know, base and odious as it is at present, that it will one day, if I be worthy, be raised incorruptible and altogether beautiful and glorious. This I know; this, by your grace, I will ever keep before me.

O my God, teach me so to live, as one who believes the great dignity, the great sanctity of that material frame in which you have lodged me. And therefore, O my dear Savior, do I come so often and so earnestly to be partaker of your Body and Blood, that by means of your own ineffable holiness I may be made holy. O my Lord Jesus, I know what is written, that our bodies are the temples of the Holy Spirit. Should I not venerate that which you miraculously feed, and which your coequal Spirit inhabits? O my God, who was nailed to the Cross, "pierce you my flesh with your fear," crucify my soul and body in all that is sinful in them, and make me pure as you are pure.

21

God Alone

Thomas says to him, "My Lord and my God" (John 20:28).

I adore you, O my God, with Thomas; and if I have, like him, sinned through unbelief, I adore you the more. I adore you as the One adorable, I adore you as more glorious in your humiliation, when men despised you, than when angels worshipped you. My God and my all, to have you is to have everything I can have. O my eternal Father, give me yourself. I dared not have made so bold a request, it would have been presumption, unless you had encouraged me. You have put it into my mouth, you have clothed yourself in my nature, you have become my brother, you have died as other men die, only in far greater bitterness, that, instead of my eyeing you fearfully from afar, I might confidently draw near to you. You speak to me as you did to Thomas, and beckon me to take hold of you.

My God and my all, what could I say more than this, if I spoke to all eternity! I am full and abound and overflow, when I have you; but without you I am nothing—I wither away, I dissolve and perish. My Lord and my God, my God and my all, give me yourself and nothing else.

Thomas came and touched your sacred wounds. Oh, will the day ever come when I shall be allowed actually and visibly to kiss them? What a day will that be when I am thoroughly cleansed from all impurity and sin and am fit to draw near to my Incarnate God in his palace of light above! What a morning, when having done with all penal suffering, I see you for the first time with these very eyes of mine, I see your countenance, gaze upon your eyes and gracious lips without quailing, and then kneel down with joy to kiss your feet, and am welcomed into your arms. O my only true lover, the only lover of my soul, you will I love now, that I may love you then. What a day, a long day without ending, the day of eternity, when I shall be so unlike what I am now, when I feel in myself a body of death, and am perplexed and distracted with ten thousand thoughts, any one of which would keep me from heaven. O my Lord, what a day when I shall have done once for all with all sins, venial as well as mortal, and shall stand perfect and acceptable in your sight, able to bear your presence, not shrinking from your eye, not shrinking from the pure scrutiny of angels and archangels, when I stand in the midst and they around me!

O my God, though I am not fit to see or touch you yet, still I will ever come within your reach, and desire that which is not yet given me in its fullness. O my Savior, you shall be my sole God! I will have no Lord but you. I will break to pieces all idols in my heart that rival you. I will have nothing but Jesus and him crucified. It shall be my life to pray to you, to offer myself to you, to keep you before me, to worship you in your holy Sacrifice, and to surrender myself to you in Holy Communion.

22

The Forbearance of Jesus

I adore you, O my Lord, for your wonderful patience and your compassionate tenderhearted condescension. Your disciples, in spite of all your teaching and miracles, disbelieved you when they saw you die and fled; nor did they take courage afterward or think of your promise of rising again on the third day. They did not believe Magdalene or the other women who said they had seen you alive again. Yet you appeared to them; you showed them your wounds; you let them touch you; you ate before them and gave them your peace.

O Jesus, is any obstinacy too great for your love? Does any number of falls and relapses vanquish the faithfulness and endurance of your compassion? You forgive not only seven times, but to seventy times seven. Many waters cannot quench a love like yours. And such you are all over the earth, even to the end—forgiving, sparing, forbearing, waiting, though sinners are ever provoking you; pitying and taking into account their ignorance, visiting all men, all your enemies, with the gentle pleadings of your grace, day after day, year after year, up to the hour of their death—for he knows whereof we are made; he knows we are but dust.

My God, what have you done for me! Men say of you, O my only Good, that your judgments are severe and your punishments excessive. All I can say is that I have not found them so in my own case. Let others speak for themselves, and you will meet and overcome them to their own confusion in the day of reckoning. With them I have nothing to do—you will settle with them—but for me the only experience that I have is your dealings with myself, and here I bear witness, as I know so entirely and feel so intimately, that to me you have been nothing but forbearance and mercy. Oh, how you forget that I have ever rebelled against you! Again and again you help me. I fall, yet you do not cast me off. In spite of all my sins, you still love me, prosper me, comfort me, surround me with blessings, sustain me, and further me. I grieve your good grace, yet you give more. I insult you, yet you do not take offense, but are as kind as if I had nothing to explain, to repent of, to amend—as if I were your best, most faithful, most steady and loyal friend. And alas! I am even led to presume upon your love; it is so like easiness and indulgence, though I ought to fear you. I confess it, O my true Savior, every day is but a fresh memorial of your unwearied, unconquerable love!

O my God, suffer me still, bear with me in spite of my waywardness, perverseness, and ingratitude! I improve very slowly, but really I am moving on to heaven, or at least I wish to move. I am putting you before me, vile sinner as I am, and I am really thinking in earnest of saving my soul. Give me time to collect my thoughts and make one good effort. I protest I will put off this languor and lukewarmness. I will shake myself from this sullenness and despondency and gloom. I will rouse myself and be cheerful and walk in your light. I will have no hope or joy but you. Only give me your grace, meet me with your grace. I will through your grace do what I can, and you shall perfect it for me. Then I shall have happy days in your presence, and in the sight and adoration of your five sacred wounds.

23

The Familiarity of Jesus

The holy Baptist was separated from the world. He was a Nazarite. He went out from the world, placed himself over against it, spoke to it from his vantage ground, and called it to repentance. Then went out all Jerusalem to him into the desert, and he confronted it face-to-face. But in his teaching he spoke of one who should come to them and speak to them in a far different way. He should not separate himself from them, he should not display himself as some higher being, but as their brother, as of their flesh and of their bones, as one among many brethren, as one of the multitude and amid them; nay, he was among them already. *Medius vestrum stetit, quem vos nescitis* — "There hath stood in the midst of you, whom you know not" (John 1:26).

That greater one called himself the Son of man. He was content to be taken as ordinary in all respects, though he was the Highest. St. John and the other evangelists, though so different in the character of their accounts of him, agree most strikingly here. The Baptist says, "There is in the midst of you One whom you know not." Next we read of his pointing Jesus out privately, not to crowds, but to one or two of his own religious followers; then of their seeking Jesus and being allowed to follow him home. At length Jesus begins to disclose himself and to manifest his glory in miracles; but where? At a marriage feast, where there was often excess, as the steward implies. And how? In adding to the wine, the instrument of such excess, when it occurred. He was at that marriage feast not as a teacher, but as a guest, and (so to speak) in a social way, for he was with his mother.

Now compare this with what he says in St. Matthew's Gospel of himself: "John came neither eating nor drinking—The Son of man came eating and drinking, and they say: Behold a man that is a glutton and wine-drinker" (Matt. 11:19). John might be hated, but he was respected; Jesus was despised. See also Mark 1:22, 27, 37, and 3:21 for the astonishment and rudeness of all about him. The objection occurs *at once*, 2:16.[1] What a marked

---

[1] And the scribes of the Pharisees, when they saw that he was eating with sinners and tax collectors, said to his disciples, "Why does he eat with tax collectors and sinners?"

feature it must have been of our Lord's character and mission, since two evangelists, so independent in their narrations, record it!

This was, O dear Lord, because you so love this human nature which you have created. You did not love us merely as your creatures, the work of your hands, but as men. You love all, for you have created all; but you love man more than all. How is it, Lord, that this should be? What is there in man, above others? Quid est homo, quod memor es ejus?—"What is man, that you are mindful of him?" (Ps. 8:4).

Who can sound the depth of your counsels and decrees? You have loved man more than you have loved the angels: and therefore, as you did not take on you an angelic nature when you manifested yourself for our salvation, so too you would not come in any shape or capacity or office that was above the course of ordinary human life—not as a Nazarene, not as a Levitical priest, not as a monk, not as a hermit, but in the fullness and exactness of that human nature which you so much love. You came not only a perfect man, but as proper man; not formed anew out of earth, not with the spiritual body that you now have, but in that very flesh which had fallen in Adam, with all our infirmities, all our feelings and sympathies, sin excepted.

The Familiarity of Jesus

O Jesus, it became you, the great God, thus abundantly and largely to do your work, for which the Father sent you. You did not do it by halves—and, while that magnificence of sacrifice is your glory as God, it is our consolation and aid as sinners. O dearest Lord, you are more fully man than the holy Baptist, than St. John, apostle and evangelist, than your own sweet mother. As in divine knowledge of me you are beyond them all, so also in experience and personal knowledge of my nature. You are my elder brother. How can I fear, how should I not repose my whole heart on one so gentle, so tender, so familiar, so unpretending, so modest, so natural, so humble? You are now, though in heaven, just the same as you were on earth: the mighty God, yet the little child—the all-holy, yet the all-sensitive, all-human.

24

Jesus, the Hidden God

"Be not faithless, but believing" (John 20:27).

I adore you, O my God, who are so awesome, because you are hidden and unseen! I adore you, and I desire to live by faith in what I do not see; and considering what I am, a disinherited outcast, I think it has indeed gone well with me that I am allowed, O my unseen Lord and Savior, to worship you anyhow. O my God, I know that it is sin that has separated you from me. I know it is sin that has brought on me the penalty of ignorance. Adam, before he fell, was visited by angels. Your saints, too, who keep close to you, see visions, and in many ways are brought into sensible perception of your presence. But to a sinner such as I am, what is left but to possess you without seeing you?

Ah, should I not rejoice at having that most extreme mercy and favor of possessing you at all? It is sin that has reduced me to live by faith, as I must at best, and should I not rejoice in such a life, O Lord my God? I see and know, O my good Jesus, that the only way in which I can possibly approach you in this world is the way of faith, faith in what you have told me, and I thankfully follow this only way which you have given me.

O my God, you over-abound in mercy! To live by faith is my necessity, from my present state of being and from my sin; but you have pronounced a blessing on it. You have said that I am more blessed if I believe in you than if I saw you. Give me to share that blessedness; give it to me in its fullness. Enable me to believe as if I saw; let me have you always before me as if you were always bodily and sensibly present. Let me ever hold communion with you, my hidden, but my living God. You are in my innermost heart. You are the life of my life. Every breath I breathe, every thought of my mind, every good desire of my heart is from the presence within me of the unseen God. By nature and by grace you are in me. I see you not in the material world except dimly, but I recognize your voice in my own intimate consciousness. I turn around and say *Rabboni* (cf. John 20:16). Oh, be ever thus with me; and if I am tempted to leave you, do not you, O my God, leave me.

O my dear Savior, would that I had any right to ask to be allowed to make reparation to you for all the unbelief of the world, and all the insults offered to your Name, your Word, your Church, and the Sacrament of your love! But, alas, I have a long score of unbelief and ingratitude of my own to atone for. You are in the sacrifice of the Mass, you are in the tabernacle, verily and indeed, in flesh and blood; and the world not only disbelieves, but mocks at this gracious truth. You warned us long ago by yourself and by your apostles that you would hide yourself from the world. The prophecy is fulfilled more than ever now; but I know what the world knows not. Oh, accept my homage, my praise, my adoration! Let me at least not be found wanting. I cannot help the sins of others—but one at least of those whom you have redeemed shall turn around and with a loud voice glorify God. The more men scoff, the more will I believe in you, the good God, the good Jesus, the hidden Lord of life, who have done me nothing else but good from the very first moment that I began to live.

25

Jesus, the Light of the Soul

"Stay with us, because it is towards evening" (Luke 24:29).

I adore you, O my God, as the true and only light! From eternity to eternity, before any creature was, when you were alone, alone but not solitary, for you have ever been three in one; you were the infinite light. There was none to see you but yourself. The Father saw that light in the Son, and the Son in the Father. Such as you were in the beginning, such you are now: most separate from all creatures in this your uncreated brightness, most glorious, most beautiful. Your attributes are so many separate and resplendent colors, each as perfect in its own purity and grace as if it were the sole and highest perfection.

Nothing created is more than the very shadow of you. Bright as are the angels, they are poor and most unworthy shadows of you. They pale and look dim and gather blackness before you. They are so feeble beside you that they are unable to gaze upon you. The highest seraphim veil their eyes, by deed as well as by word proclaiming your unutterable glory. For me, I cannot even look upon the sun, and what is this but a base material emblem of you? How should I endure to look on even an angel? And how could I look upon you and live? If I were placed in the illumination of your countenance, I would shrink up like the grass. O most gracious God, who shall approach you, being so glorious, yet how can I keep from you?

How can I keep from you? For you, who are the light of angels, are the only light of my soul. You enlighten every man that cometh into this world. I am utterly dark, as dark as hell, without you. I droop and shrink when you are away. I revive only in proportion as you dawn upon me. You come and go at your will. O my God, I cannot keep you! I can only beg of you to stay. *Mane nobiscum, Domine, quoniam advesperascit* (Luke 24:29). Remain until morning, and then go not without giving me a blessing. Remain with me till death in this dark valley, when the darkness will end. Remain, O light of my soul, *jam advesperascit!* The gloom, which is not yours, falls over me. I am nothing. I have little command of myself. I cannot do what I would. I am disconsolate and sad. I want something; I know not what. It is you that I want, though I so little understand this. I say it and take it on faith; I partially understand it, but very poorly. Shine on me "O fire ever burning and never failing," and I shall begin, through and in your light, to see light and to recognize you truly, as the source of light. *Mane nobiscum*. Stay, sweet Jesus; stay forever. In this decay of nature, give more grace.

Stay with me, and then I shall begin to shine as you shine: so to shine as to be a light to others. The light, O Jesus, will be all from you. None of it will be mine. No merit to me. It will be you who shine through me upon others. Oh, let me thus praise you, in the way you love best, by shining on all those around me. Give light to them as well as to me; light them with me, through me. Teach me to show forth your praise, your truth, your will. Make me preach you without preaching—not by words, but by my example and by the catching force, the sympathetic influence, of what I do—by my visible resemblance to your saints, and the evident fullness of the love which my heart bears to you.

26

God Is All-Sufficient

"Show us the Father, and it is enough for us. . . . he that seeth me, seeth the Father also" (John 14:8–9).

The Son is in the Father and the Father in the Son. O adorable mystery that has been from eternity! I adore you, O my incomprehensible Creator, before whom I am an atom, a being of yesterday or an hour ago! Go back a few years, and I simply did not exist; I was not in being, and things went on without me; but you are from eternity; and nothing whatever for one moment could go on without you. And from eternity too you have possessed your nature; you have been — this awesome glorious mystery — the Son in the Father and the Father in the Son. Whether we exist, or whether we do not, you are one and the same always, the Son sufficient for the Father, the Father for the Son — and all other things, in themselves, but vanity. All things once were not, all things might not be, but it would be enough for the Father that he had begotten his coequal consubstantial Son, and for the Son that he was embraced in the bosom of the eternal Father. O adorable mystery! Human reason has not conducted me to it, but I believe. I believe, because you have spoken, O Lord. I joyfully accept your word about yourself. You must know what you are—and who else? Not I surely, dust and ashes, except so far as you tell me. I take then your own witness, O my Creator, and I believe firmly, I repeat after you, what I do not understand, because I wish to live a life of faith; and I prefer faith in you to trust in myself.

O my great God, from eternity you were sufficient for yourself! The Father was sufficient for the Son, and the Son for the Father; are you not then sufficient for me, a poor creature, you so great, I so little! I have a double all-sufficiency in the Father and the Son. I will take then St. Philip's word and say: Show us the Father, and it *suffices* us. It suffices us, for then are we full to overflowing, when we have you. O mighty God, strengthen me with your strength, console me with your everlasting peace, soothe me with the beauty of your countenance; enlighten me with your uncreated brightness; purify me with the fragrance of your ineffable holiness. Bathe me in yourself, and give me to drink, as far as mortal man may ask, of the rivers of grace that flow from the Father and the Son, the grace of your consubstantial, coeternal love.

O my God, let me never forget this truth: that not only are you my life, but my only life! You are the way, the truth, and the life. You are my life, and the life of all who live. All men, all I know, all I meet, all I see and hear of, live not unless they live by you. They live in you, or else they live not at all. No one can be saved outside of you. Let me never forget this in the business of the day. Oh, give me a true love of souls, of those souls for whom you died. Teach me to pray for their conversion, to do my part toward effecting it. However able they are, however amiable, however high and distinguished, they cannot be saved unless they have you. O my all-sufficient Lord, you alone suffice. Your blood is sufficient for the whole world. As you are sufficient for me, so you are sufficient for the entire race of Adam. O my Lord Jesus, let your Cross be more than sufficient for them; let it be effectual! Let it be effectual for me more than all, lest I have all and abound, yet bring no fruit to perfection.

27

God Alone Is Unchangeable

"Whither I go, you cannot follow me now, but you shall follow hereafter" (John 13:36).

You alone, O my God, are what you ever have been! Man changes. You are unchangeable; nay, even as man you have ever been unchangeable, for Jesus is yesterday and today himself, and forever. Your word endures in heaven and earth. Your decrees are fixed; your gifts are without repentance. Your nature, your attributes, are ever the same. There ever was Father, ever Son, ever Holy Spirit. I adore you in the peace and serenity of your unchangeableness. I adore you in that imperturbable heaven, which is yourself. You were perfect from the first; nothing could you gain, and nothing might you lose. There was nothing that could touch you, because there was nothing but what you did create and could destroy. Again, I adore you in this your infinite stability, which is the center and stay of all created things.

Man on the contrary is ever changing. Not a day passes but I am nearer the grave. Whatever be my age, whatever the number of my years, I am ever narrowing the interval between time and eternity. I am ever changing in myself. Youth is not like age; and I am continually changing, as I pass along out of youth toward the end of life. O my God, I am crumbling away, as I go on! I am already dissolving into my first elements. My soul indeed cannot die, for you have made it immortal; but my bodily frame is continually resolving into that dust out of which it was taken. All below heaven changes: spring, summer, autumn; each has its turn. The fortunes of the world change; what was high lies low; what was low rises high. Riches take wings and flee away; bereavements happen. Friends become enemies, and enemies friends. Our wishes, aims, and plans change. There is nothing stable but you, O my God! And you are the center and life of all, who change, who trust you as their Father, who look to you, and who are content to put themselves into your hands.

I know, O my God, I must change, if I am to see your face! I must undergo the change of death. Body and soul must die to this world. My real self, my soul, must change by a true regeneration. None but the holy can see you. Like Peter, I cannot have a blessing now, which I shall have afterward. "You cannot follow me now, but you shall follow hereafter." Oh, support me, as I proceed in this great, awful, happy change, with the grace of your unchangeableness. My unchangeableness here below is perseverance in changing. Let me day by day be molded upon you, and be changed from glory to glory, by ever looking toward you, and ever leaning on your arm. I know, O Lord, I must go through trial, temptation, and much conflict, if I am to come to you. I know not what lies before me, but I know as much as this. I know, too, that if you are not with me, my change will be for the worse, not for the better. Whatever fortune I have, be I rich or poor, healthy or sick, with friends or without, all will turn to evil if I am not sustained by the Unchangeable; all will turn to good if I have Jesus with me, yesterday and today the same, and forever.

28

God Is Love

Jesus saith to him, "Love you me more than these?" (John 21:15).

You ask us to love you, O my God, and you are yourself love. There was one attribute of yours that you exercised from eternity, and that was love. We hear of no exercise of your power while you were alone, nor of your justice before there were creatures on their trial; nor of your wisdom before the acts and works of your providence; but from eternity you loved, for you are not only one but three. The Father loved from eternity his only-begotten Son, and the Son returned to him an equal love; and the Holy Spirit is that love in substance, wherewith the Father and the Son love one another. This, O Lord, is your ineffable and special blessedness. It is love. I adore you, O my infinite Love!

And when you had created us, then you did but love more, if that were possible. You loved not only your own coequal Self in the multiplied personality of the God-head, but you loved your creatures also. You were love to us, as well as love in yourself. You were love to man, more than to any other creatures. It was love that brought you from heaven, and subjected you to the laws of a created nature. It was love alone that was able to conquer you, the Highest—and bring you low. You died through your infinite love of sinners. And it is love that keeps you here still, even now that you have ascended on high, in a small tabernacle and under cheap and common outward forms. O *Amor meus*, if you were not infinite love, would you remain here, one hour, imprisoned and exposed to slight, indignity, and insult? O my God, I do not know what infinity means, but one thing I see: that you are loving to a depth and height far beyond any measurement of mine.

And now you bid me love you in turn, for you have loved me. You woo me to love, to love you specially, above others. You ask, "Love you me more than these?" O my God, how shameful that such a question need be put to me! Yet, after all, do I really love you more than the run of men? The run of men do not really love you at all, but put you out of their thoughts. They feel it un-pleasant to them to think of you; they have no sort of heart for you yet. You have need to ask me whether I love you even a little. Why should I not love you much; how can I help loving you much, whom you have brought so near to yourself, whom you have so wonderfully chosen out of the world to be your own special servant and son? Have I not cause to love you abundantly more than others, though all ought to love you? I do not know what you have done for others personally — though you have died for all — but I know what you have done especially for me. You have done that for me, O my Love, which ought to make me love you with all my powers.

29

The Sanctity of God

You are holy, O Lord, in that you are infinitely separate from everything but yourself and incommunicable.

I adore you, O Lord, in this your proper sanctity and everlasting purity, for that all your blessedness comes from within, and nothing touches you from without. I adore you as infinitely blessed, yet having all your blessedness in yourself. I adore you in that perfect and most holy knowledge of yourself, in which we conceive the generation of the Word.

I adore you in that infinite and most pure love of yourself, a love of your Son, and your Son's love for you, in which we conceive the procession of the Holy Spirit. I adore you in that blessedness which you possessed in yourself from all eternity.

My God, I do not understand these heavenly things. I use words I cannot master; but I believe to be true, O God, that which I thus feebly express in human language.

My God, I adore you, as holy without, as well as holy within. I adore you as holy in all your works as well as in your own nature. No creature can approach your incommunicable sanctity, but you approach, and touch, and compass, and possess, all creatures; and nothing lives but in you, and you have created nothing but what is good. I adore you, as having made everything good after its kind. I adore you, as having infused your preserving and sustaining power into all things, while you did create them, so that they continue to live, though you do not touch them, and do not crumble back into nothing. I adore you, as having put real power into them, so that they are able to act, though from you and with you and yet of themselves. I adore you as having given power to will what is right, and your holy grace to your rational creatures. I adore you as having created man upright, and having bountifully given him an integrity of nature, and having filled him with your free grace, so that he was like an angel upon earth; and I adore you still more, for having given him your grace over again in still more copious measure, and with far more lasting fruits, through your eternal Son incarnate. In all your works you are holy, O my God, and I adore you in them all.

Holy are you in all your works, O Lord, and if there is sin in the world it is not from you — it is from an enemy;

it is from me and mine. To me, to man, be the shame, for we might will what is right, and yet we will what is evil. What a gulf is there between you and me, O my Creator—not only as to nature but as to will! Your will is ever holy. How, O Lord, shall I ever dare approach you? What have I to do with you? Yet I must approach you; you will call me to you when I die and judge me. Woe is me, for I am a man of unclean lips, and dwell in the midst of a people of unclean lips! (Isa. 6:5). Your Cross, O Lord, shows the distance that is between you and me, while it takes it away. It shows both my great sinfulness and your utter abhorrence of sin. Impart to me, my dear Lord, the doctrine of the Cross in its fullness, that it may not only teach me my alienation from you, but convey to me the virtue of your reconciliation.

30

The Kingdom of God

O my Lord Jesus, how wonderful were those conversations you held from time to time with your disciples after your Resurrection. When you went with two of them to Emmaus, you explained all the prophecies that related to you. And you committed to the Apostles the sacraments in fullness, the truths which it was your will to reveal, and the principles and maxims by which your Church was to be maintained and governed. Thus you did prepare them for the day of Pentecost (as the risen bodies were put into shape for the Spirit in the prophet's vision [cf. Ezek. 37:1–14]), when life and illumination were to be infused into them.

I will think over all you said to them with a true and simple faith. The kingdom of God was your sacred subject. Let me never for an instant forget that you have established on earth a kingdom of your own, that the Church is your work, your establishment, your instrument; that we are under your rule, your laws and your eye; that when the Church speaks, you speak. Let not familiarity with this wonderful truth lead me to be insensible to it — let not the weakness of your human representatives lead me to forget that it is you who speaks and acts through them. It was just when you were going away that you left this kingdom of yours to take your place until the end of the world, to speak for you, as your visible form, when your personal presence, sensible to man, was departing. I will in true loving faith bring you before me, teaching all the truths and laws of this kingdom to your apostles, and I will adore you, while in my thoughts I gaze upon you and listen to your words.

Come, O my dear Lord, and teach me in like manner. I need it not, and do not ask it, as far as this, that the word of truth which in the beginning was given to the Apostles by you, has been handed down from age to age and has already been taught to me, and your infallible Church is the warrant of it. But I need you to teach me day by day, according to each day's opportunities and needs. I need you to give me that true divine instinct about revealed matters that, knowing one part, I may be able to antici-pate or to approve of others. I need that understanding of the truths about yourself which may prepare me for all your other truths — or at least may save me from conjecturing wrongly about them or commenting falsely upon them. I need the mind of the Spirit, which is the mind of the holy Fathers, and of the Church, by which I may not only say what they say on definite points, but think what they think; in all I need to be saved from an originality of thought, which is not true if it leads away from you. Give me the gift of discriminating between true and false in all discourse of mind.

And, for that end, give me, O my Lord, that purity of conscience which alone can receive, which alone can improve your inspirations. My ears are dull, so that I cannot hear your voice. My eyes are dim, so that I cannot see your tokens. You alone can quicken my hearing, and purge my sight, and cleanse and renew my heart. Teach me, like Mary, to sit at your feet, and to hear your word. Give me that true wisdom which seeks your will by prayer and meditation, by direct communion with you, more than by reading and reasoning. Give me the discernment to know your voice from the voices of strangers, and to rest upon it and to seek it in the first place, as something external to myself; and answer me through my own mind, if I worship and rely on you as above and beyond it.

31

Resignation to God's Will

"What is it to you? Follow you me" (John 21:22).

O my God, you and you alone are all wise and all knowing! You know, you have determined everything that will happen to us from first to last. You have ordered things in the wisest way, and you know what will be my lot year by year until I die. You know how long I have to live. You know how I shall die. You have precisely ordained everything, sin excepted. Every event of my life is the best for me that could be, for it comes from you. You bring me on year by year, by your wonderful Providence, from youth to age, with the most perfect wisdom, and with the most perfect love.

My Lord, who came into this world to do your Father's will, not your own, give me a most absolute and simple submission to the will of Father and Son. I believe, O my Savior, that you know just what is best for me. I believe that you love me better than I love myself, that you are all wise in your Providence and all powerful in your protection. I am as ignorant as Peter was regarding what is to happen to me in time to come; but I resign myself entirely to my ignorance, and I thank you with all my heart that you have taken me out of my own keeping, and, instead of putting such a serious charge upon me, have bidden me put myself into your hands. I can ask nothing better than this, to be your care, not my own. I protest, O my Lord, that, through your grace, I will follow you wherever you go and will not lead the way. I will wait on you for your guidance, and, on obtaining it, I will act upon it in simplicity and without fear. And I promise that I will not be impatient, if at any time I am kept by you in darkness and perplexity; nor will I ever complain or fret if I come into any misfortune or anxiety.

I know, O Lord, you will do your part toward me, as I, through your grace, desire to do my part toward you. I know well you never can forsake those who seek you or can disappoint those who trust you. Yet I know too, the more I pray for your protection, the more surely and fully I shall have it. And therefore now I cry out to you and entreat you, first that you would keep me from myself, and from following any will but yours. Next I beg of you, that in your infinite compassion, you would temper your will to me, that it may not be severe, but indulgent to me.

Resignation to God's Will

Do not visit me, O my loving Lord — if it be not wrong so to pray — do not visit me with those trying visitations which saints alone can bear! Pity my weakness, and lead me heavenward in a safe and tranquil course. Still I leave all in your hands, my dear Savior. I bargain for nothing, only, if you shall bring heavier trials on me, give me more grace, flood me with the fullness of your strength and consolation, that they may work in me not death, but life and salvation.

32

Our Lord's Parting with His Apostles

I adore you, O my God, together with your Apostles, during the forty days in which you visited them after your Resurrection. So blessed was the time, so calm, so undisturbed from without, that it was good to be there with you, and when it was over, they could hardly believe that it was more than begun. How quickly must that first *Tempus Paschale* have flown! And they perhaps hardly knew when it was to end. At least, they did not like to anticipate its ending but were engrossed with the joy of the present moment. Oh, what a time of consolation! What a contrast to what had lately taken place! It was their happy time on earth — the foretaste of heaven, not noticed, not interfered with, by man. They passed it in wonder, in musing, in adoration, rejoicing in your light, O my risen God!

But you, O my dear Lord, did know better than they! They hoped and desired, perhaps fancied, that that resting time never would end until it was superseded by something better; but you knew, in your eternal wisdom, that, in order to arrive at what was higher than any blessing that they were then enjoying, it was fitting, it was necessary, that they should sustain conflict and suffering. You knew well that unless you had departed, the Paraclete could not have come to them; and therefore you did go, that they might gain more by your sorrowful absence than by your sensible visitations. I adore you, O Father, for sending the Son and the Holy Spirit! I adore you, O Son, and you, O Holy Spirit, for vouchsafing to be sent to us!

O my God, let me never forget that seasons of consolation are refreshments here, and nothing more, not our abiding state. They will not remain with us except in heaven. Here they are only intended to prepare us for doing and suffering. I pray you, O my God, to give them to me from time to time. Shed over me the sweetness of your presence, lest I faint by the way; lest I find religious service wearisome, through my exceeding infirmity, and give over prayer and meditation; lest I go about my daily work in a dry spirit, or am tempted to take pleasure in it for its own sake, and not for you.

Give me your divine consolations from time to time; but let me not rest in them. Let me use them for the purpose for which you give them. Let me not think it grievous; let me not be downcast, if they go. Let them carry me forward to the thought and the desire of heaven.

33

God's Ways Are Not Our Ways

"Because I have spoken these things to you, sorrow has filled your heart. But I tell you the truth: it is expedient for you" (John 16:7).

O my Savior, I adore you for your infinite wisdom, which sees what we do not see and orders all things in its own most perfect way.

When you said to the Apostles that you were going away, they cried out, as if you had, if it may be so said, broken faith with them. They seemed to say to you, "O Jesus, did we not leave all things for you? Did we not give up home and family, father and wife, friends and neighbors, our habits, our accustomed way of living, that we might join you? Did we not divorce ourselves from the world, or rather die to it, that we might be eternally united and live to you? And now you say that you are leaving us. Is this reasonable? Is this just? Is this faithfulness to your promise? Did we bargain for this? O Lord

Jesus, we adore you, but we are confounded, and we know not what to say!"

Yet let God be true, and every man a liar. Let the Divine Word triumph in our minds over every argument and persuasion of sensible appearances. Let faith rule us and not sight. You are justified, O Lord, when you are arraigned, and you gain the cause when you are judged. For you knew that the true way of possessing you was to lose you. You knew that what man stands most of all in need of, and in the first place, is not an outward guide, though that he needs too, but an inward, intimate, invisible aid. You intended to heal him thoroughly, not slightly; not merely to reform the surface, but to remove and destroy the heart and root of all his ills. You then purposed to visit his soul, and you departed in body, that you might come again to him in spirit. You did not stay with your Apostles therefore, as in the days of your flesh, but you did come to them and abide with them forever, with a much more immediate and true communion in the power of the Paraclete.

O my God, in your sight, I confess and bewail my extreme weakness, in distrusting, if not you, at least your own servants and representatives, when things do not turn out as I would have them, or expected! You have given me St. Philip, that great creation of your grace, for my master and patron, and I have committed myself to him; and he has done very great things for me, and has in many ways fulfilled toward me all that I can fairly reckon he had promised. But, because in some things he has dis-appointed me, and delayed, I have gotten impatient and have served him, though without conscious disloyalty, with peevishness and coldness. O my dear Lord, give me a generous faith in you and in your servants!

34

He Ascended into Heaven

My Lord, I follow you up to heaven; as you go up, my heart
and mind go with you. Never was triumph like this. You
appeared a babe in human flesh at Bethlehem. That flesh,
taken from the Blessed Virgin, was not before you formed
it into a body; it was a new work of your hands. And your
soul was new altogether, created by your omnipotence,
at the moment when you entered into her sacred breast.
That pure soul and body, taken as a garment for yourself,
began on earth, and never had been elsewhere. This is
the triumph. Earth rises to heaven. I see you going up. I
see that form which hung upon the Cross, those scarred
hands and feet, that pierced side; they are mounting up
to heaven. And the angels are full of jubilee; the myriads
of blessed spirits, which people the glorious expanse, part
like the waters to let you pass. And the living pavement
of God's palaces is cleft in twain, and the cherubim with
flaming swords, who form the rampart of heaven against

fallen man, give way and open out, that you may enter, and your saints after you. O memorable day!

O memorable day! The Apostles feel it to be so, now that it is come, though they felt so differently before it came. When it was coming they dreaded it. They could not think but it would be a great bereavement; but now, as we read, they returned to Jerusalem "with great joy" (Luke 24:52). Oh, what a time of triumph! They understood it now. They understood how weak it had been in them to grudge their Lord and Master, the glorious captain of their salvation, the champion and first fruits of the human family, this crown of his great work. It was the triumph of redeemed man. It is the completion of his redemption. It was the last act, making the whole sure, for now man is actually in heaven. He has entered into possession of his inheritance. The sinful race has now one of its own children there, its own flesh and blood, in the person of the eternal Son. Oh, what a wonderful marriage between heaven and earth! It began in sorrow; but now the long travail of that mysterious wedding day is over; the marriage feast is begun; marriage and birth have gone together; man is newly born when Emmanuel enters heaven.

I adore you, Son of Mary, Jesus Emmanuel, my God and my Savior. I am allowed to adore you, my Savior and my own brother, for you are God. I follow you in my thoughts, O you first fruits of our race, as I hope one day by your grace to follow you in my person. To go to heaven is to go to God. God is there and God alone: for perfect bliss is there and nothing else, and none can be blessed who is not bathed and hidden and absorbed in the glory of the divine nature. All holy creatures are but the vestment of the Highest, which he has put on forever, and which is bright with his uncreated light. There are many things on earth, and each is its own center, but one name alone is named above. It is God alone. This is that true supernatural life; and if I would live a supernatural life on earth, and attain to the supernatural eternal life which is in heaven, I have one thing to do: to live on the thought of God here. Teach me this, O God; give me your supernatural grace to practice it; to have my reason, affections, intentions, aims all penetrated and possessed by the love of you, plunged and drowned in the one vision of you.

There is but one name and one thought above: there are many thoughts below. This is the earthly life, which leads to death: to follow the numberless objects and aims and toils and amusements which men pursue on earth. Even the good that is here below does not lead to heaven; it is spoilt in the selling; it perishes in the using; it has no stay, no integrity, no consistency. It runs off into evil before it has well ceased, before it has well begun to be good. It is at best vanity, when it is nothing worse. It has in it commonly the seeds of real sin. My God, I acknowledge all this. My Lord Jesus, I confess and know that you only are the true, the beautiful, and the good. You alone can make me bright and glorious and can lead me up after you. You are the way, the truth, and the life, and none but you. Earth will never lead me to heaven. You alone are the way; you alone.

My God, shall I for one moment doubt where my path lies? Shall I not at once take you for my portion? To whom should I go? You have the words of eternal life (cf. John 6:68). You came down for the very purpose of doing that which no one here below could do for me. None but he who is in heaven can bring me to heaven. What strength have I to scale the high mountain? Though I served the world ever so well, though I did my duty in it (as men speak), what could the world do for me, however hard it tried? Though I filled my station well, did good to my fellows, had a fair name or a wide reputation, though I did great deeds and was celebrated, though I had the praise of history, how would all this bring me to heaven? I choose you then for my one portion, because you live and die not. I cast away all idols. I give myself to *you*. I pray you to teach me, guide me, enable me, and receive me to you.

35

Our Advocate Above

I adore you, O Lord, as is most fitting, for you are gone to heaven to take my part there and defend my interests. I have one to plead for me with the Lord of all. On earth we try to put ourselves under the protection of powerful men when we have any important business on hand; we know the value of their influence, and we make much of any promise they make us. You are omnipotent, and you exert your omnipotence for me.

There are millions of men in the world. You died for them all, but you live for your people, whom you have chosen out of the world. And still more marvelously do you live for your predestinate. You have engraved them upon the palms of your hands; their names are ever before you. You count the full roll of them; you know them by heart. You order the crown of the world for them; and, when their number shall be completed, the world shall end.

For me, you have chosen me for present grace, and thus you have put me in the way for future glory. I know perfectly well that, whatever be your secret counsels about me, it will be simply, entirely, most really my own fault if I am not written in your book. I cannot understand you. I can understand myself enough to know and be sure of this. You have put me on such a special ground that the prize is almost in my hand. If I am at present in the society of angels or saints, it is hard if I cannot make interest with them that the fellowship begun between them and me should endure. Men of the world know how to turn such opportunities to account in their own matters. If you have given me Mary for my mother, who, O my God, is yours, cannot I now establish, as it were, a family interest in her, so that she will not cast me off at the last? If I have the right to pray, may I not thereby secure that perseverance to the end, which I cannot merit, and which is the sign and assurance of my predestination? I have in my hands all the means of that which I have not and may infallibly obtain, even though I cannot certainly secure it.

O my Lord, I sink down almost in despair, in utter remorse certainly and disgust at myself, that I so utterly neglect these means which you have put into my hands, content to let things take their course, as if grace would infallibly lead to glory without my own trouble in the matter. What shall I say to you, O my Savior, except that I am in the chains of habit, feeble, helpless, stunted, growthless, and as if I were meant to walk through life, as the inferior creatures, with my face down to the earth, on hands and feet, or crawling on, instead of having an erect posture and a heavenward face? Come give me what I need: contrition for all those infinitely numerous venial sins, negligences, slovenliness, which are the surest foreboding that I am not of your predestinate. Who can save me from myself but you?

I cannot penetrate your secret decrees, O Lord! I know you died for all men really; but since you have not effectually willed the salvation of all, and since you might have done so, it is certain that you do for one what you do not do for another. I cannot tell what has been your everlasting purpose about myself, but, if I go by all the signs you have lavished upon me, I may hope that I am one of those whose names are written in your book. But this I know and feel most entirely, what I believe in the case of all men but know and feel in my own case: that, if I do not attain to that crown which I see and which is within my reach, it is entirely my own fault. You have surrounded me from childhood with your mercies; you have taken as much pains with me as if I was of importance to you, and my loss of heaven would be your loss of me. You have led me on by ten thousand merciful providences. You have brought me near to you in the most intimate of ways. You have brought me into your house and chamber. You have fed me with yourself. Do you not love me, really, truly, substantially, efficaciously love me, without any limitation of the word? I know it. I have an utter conviction of it. You are ever waiting to do me benefits, to pour upon me blessings. You are ever waiting for me to ask you to be merciful to me.

Yes, my Lord, you do desire that I should ask you. You are ever listening for my voice. There is nothing I cannot get from you. I confess my heinous neglect of this great privilege. I am very guilty. I have trifled with the highest of gifts, the power to move Omnipotence. How slack am I in praying to you for my own needs! How little have I thought of the needs of others! How little have I brought before you the needs of the world and of your Church! How little I have asked for graces in detail and for aid in daily wants! How little have I interceded for individuals! How little have I accompanied actions and undertakings, in themselves good, with prayer for your guidance and blessing!

O my Lord Jesus, I will use the time. It will be too late to pray when life is over. There is no prayer in the grave; there is no meriting in purgatory. Low as I am in your all-holy sight, I am strong in you, strong through your Immaculate Mother, through your saints: and thus I can do much for the Church, for the world, for all I love. Oh, let not the blood of souls be on my head! Oh, let me not walk my own way without thinking of you. Let me bring everything before you, asking your leave for everything I purpose, your blessing on everything I do. I will not move without you. I will ever lift up my heart to you. I will never forget that you are my advocate at the throne of the Highest. As the dial speaks of the sun, so will I be ruled by you above, if you will take me and rule me. Be it so, my Lord Jesus. I give myself wholly to you.

36

The Paraclete, the Life of All Things

"I adore you, my Lord and God, the eternal Paraclete, co-equal with the Father and the Son. I adore you as the life of all that live. Through you the whole material universe hangs together and consists, remains in its place, and moves internally in the order and reciprocity of its several parts. Through you the earth was brought into its present state and was matured through its six days to be a habitation for man. Through you, all trees, herbs, and fruits thrive and are perfected. Through you, spring comes after winter and renews all things. That wonderful and beautiful, that irresistible burst into life again, in spite of all obstacles, that awful triumph of nature, is but your glorious presence. Through you the many tribes of brute animals live day by day, drawing in their breath from you. You are the life of the whole creation, O eternal Paraclete—and if you are the life of this animal and material framework, how much more of the world of spirits! Through you,

121

almighty Lord, the angels and saints sing your praises in heaven. Through you our own dead souls are quickened to serve you. From you is every good thought and desire, every good purpose, every good effort, every good success. It is by you that sinners are turned into saints. It is by you that the Church is refreshed and strengthened and champions start forth and martyrs are carried on to their crown. Through you new religious orders, new devotions in the Church come into being; new countries are added to the Faith; new manifestations and illustrations are given of the ancient apostolic creed. I praise and adore you, my sovereign Lord God, the Holy Spirit.

I adore you, O dread Lord, for what you have done for my soul. I acknowledge and feel, as a matter not only of faith but of experience, that I cannot have one good thought or do one good act without you. I know, that if I attempt anything good in my own strength, I shall to a certainty fail. I have bitter experience of this. My God, I am safe only when you breathe upon me. If you withdraw your breath, forthwith my three mortal enemies rush on me and overcome me. I am as weak as water; I am utterly impotent without you. The minute you cease to act in me, I begin to languish, to gasp, and to faint away. Of my good desires, whatever they may be, of my good aims, aspirations, attempts, successes, habits, practices, you are the sole cause and present continual source. I have nothing but what I have received, and I protest now in your presence, O sovereign Paraclete, that I have nothing to glory in and everything to be humbled at.

O my dear Lord, how merciful you have been to me. When I was young, you did put into my heart a special devotion to you. You have taken me up in my youth, and in my age you will not forsake me. Not for my merit, but from your free and bountiful love You put good resolutions into me when I was young and turned me to you. You will never forsake me. I earnestly trust so—never, certainly, without fearful provocation on my part. Yet I trust and pray that you will keep me from that provocation. Oh, keep me from the provocation of lukewarmness and sloth. O my dear Lord, lead me forward from strength to strength, gently, sweetly, tenderly, lovingly, powerfully, effectually, remembering my fretfulness and feebleness, until you bring me into your heaven.

37

The Paraclete, the Life of the Church

I adore you, O my Lord, the third person of the all-blessed Trinity, that you have set up in this world of sin a great light upon a hill. You have founded the Church; you have established and maintained it. You fill it continually with your gifts, that men may see, and draw near, and take, and live. You have in this way brought down heaven upon earth. For you have set up a great company which angels visit by that ladder which the patriarch saw in vision (cf. Gen. 28:10–12). You have by your presence restored the communion between God above and man below. You have given him that light of grace which is one with and the commencement of the light of glory. I adore and praise you for your infinite mercy toward us, O my Lord and God.

I adore you, almighty Lord, the Paraclete, because you in your infinite compassion have brought me into this Church, the work of your supernatural power. I had no claim on you for so wonderful a favor over anyone else in the whole world. There were many men far better than I by nature, gifted with more pleasing natural gifts, and less stained with sin. Yet you, in your inscrutable love for me, have chosen me and brought me into your fold. You have a reason for everything you do. I know there must have been an all-wise reason, as we speak in human language, for your choosing me and not another, but I know that that reason was something external to myself. I did nothing toward it—I did everything against it. I did everything to thwart your purpose. And thus I owe all to your grace. I would have lived and died in darkness and sin; I would have become worse and worse the longer I lived; I would have grown more to hate and abjure you, O source of my bliss; I would have become yearly more fit for hell, and at length I would have gone there, but for your incomprehensible love for me. O my God, that overpowering love took me captive. Was any boyhood so impious as some years of mine! Did I not in fact dare you to do your worst? Ah, how I struggled to get free from you; but you are stronger than I and have prevailed. I have not a word to say, but to bow down in awe before the depths of your love.

And then, in course of time, slowly but infallibly did your grace bring me on into your Church. Now then give me this further grace, Lord, to use all this grace well and to turn it to my salvation. Teach me, make me, to come to the fountains of mercy continually with an awakened, eager mind and with lively devotion. Give me a love of your sacraments and ordinances. Teach me to value as I ought, to prize as the inestimable pearl, that pardon which again and again you give me, and the great and heavenly gift of the presence of him whose Spirit you are, upon the altar. Without you I can do nothing, and you are there where your Church is and your sacraments. Give me grace to rest in them forever, until they are lost in the glory of your manifestation in the world to come.

38

The Paraclete, the Life of My Soul

My God, I adore you for taking on yourself the charge of sinners; of those, who not only cannot profit you, but who continually grieve and profane you. You have taken on yourself the office of a minister, and that for those who did not ask for it. I adore you for your incomprehensible condescension in ministering to me. I know and feel, O my God, that you might have left me, as I wished to be left, to go my own way, to go straight forward in my willfulness and self-trust to hell. You might have left me in that enmity to you which is in itself death. I would at length have died the second death and would have had no one to blame for it but myself. But you, O eternal Father, have been kinder to me than I am to myself. You have given me, you have poured out upon me your grace, and thus I live.

My God, I adore you, O eternal Paraclete, the light and the life of my soul. You might have been content with merely giving me good suggestions, inspiring grace, and helping from without. You might thus have led me on, cleansing me with your inward virtue, when I changed my state from this world to the next. But in your infinite compassion you have from the first entered into my soul, and taken possession of it. You have made it your temple. You dwell in me by your grace in an ineffable way, uniting me to yourself and the whole company of angels and saints. Nay, as some have held, you are present in me, not only by your grace, but by your eternal substance, as if, though I did not lose my own individuality, in some sense I was even here absorbed in God—as though you had taken possession of my very body, this earthly, fleshly, wretched tabernacle; even my body is your temple. O astonishing, awesome truth! I believe it, I know it, O my God.

O my God, can I sin when you are so intimately with me? Can I forget who is with me, who is in me? Can I expel a divine inhabitant by that which he abhors more than anything else, which is the one thing in the whole world that is offensive to him, the only thing that is not his? Would not this be a kind of sin against the Holy Spirit? My God, I have a double security against sinning: first, the dread of such a profanation of all you are to me in your very presence; and next, because I do trust that

that presence will preserve me from sin. My God, you will go from me, if I sin; and I shall be left to my own miserable self. God forbid! I will use what you have given me; I will call on you when tried and tempted. I will guard against the sloth and carelessness into which I am continually falling. Through you I will never forsake you.

39

The Paraclete, the Fount of Love

My God, I adore you, as the third person of the ever-blessed Trinity, under the name and designation of Love. You are that living love, wherewith the Father and the Son love each other. And you are the author of supernatural love in our hearts — *Fons vivus, ignis, caritas*. As a fire you came down from heaven on the day of Pentecost, and as a fire you burn away the dross of sin and vanity in the heart and light up the pure flame of devotion and affection. It is you who unites heaven and earth by showing to us the glory and beauty of the divine nature and making us love what is in itself so winning and transporting. I adore you, O uncreated and everlasting fire, by which our souls live, by which alone they are made fit for heaven.

My God, the Paraclete, I acknowledge you as the giver of that great gift, by which alone we are saved: supernatural love. Man is by nature blind and hard-hearted in all spiritual matters; how is he to reach heaven? It is by the flame of your grace, which consumes him in order to new-make him and so to fit him to enjoy what without you he would have no taste for. It is you, O almighty Para-clete, who have been and are the strength, the vigor and endurance, of the martyr in the midst of his torments. You are the stay of the confessor in his long, tedious, and humiliating toils. You are the fire by which the preacher wins souls, without thought of himself, in his mission-ary labors. By you we wake up from the death of sin, to exchange the idolatry of the creature for the pure love of the Creator. By you we make acts of faith, hope, char-ity, and contrition. By you we live in the atmosphere of earth, proof against its infection. By you we are able to consecrate ourselves to the sacred ministry, and fulfill our awful engagements to it. By the fire you kindled within us, we pray, meditate, and do penance. As well could our bodies live if the sun were extinguished, as our souls if you are away.

My most holy Lord and sanctifier, whatever there is of good in me is yours. Without you, I would but get worse and worse as years went on and would tend to be a devil. If I differ at all from the world, it is because you have cho-sen me out of the world, and have lit up the love of God in my heart. If I differ from your saints, it is because I do not ask earnestly enough for your grace, and for enough of it, and because I do not diligently improve what you have given me. Increase in me this grace of love, in spite of all my unworthiness. It is more precious than anything else in the world. I accept it in place of all the world can give me. Oh, give it to me! It is my life.

40

The Holy Sacrifice

I adore you, O Lord God, with the most profound awe for your Passion and Crucifixion, in sacrifice for our sins. You suffered incommunicable sufferings in your sinless soul. You were exposed in your innocent body to ignominious torments, to mingled pain and shame. You were stripped and fiercely scourged, your sacred body vibrating under the heavy flail as trees under the blast. You were, when thus mangled, hung upon the Cross, naked, a spectacle for all to see you quivering and dying.

What does all this imply, O mighty God! What a depth is here which we cannot fathom! My God, I know well, you could have saved us at your word, without yourself suffering; but you chose to purchase us at the price of your blood. I look on you, the victim lifted up on Calvary, and I know and protest that that death of yours was an expiation for the sins of the whole world. I believe and know that you alone could have offered a meritorious atonement; for it was your divine nature that gave your sufferings worth. Rather than I should perish according to my deserts, you were nailed to the tree and died.

Such a sacrifice was not to be forgotten. It was not to be — it could not be — a mere event in the world's history, which was to be done and over and was to pass away except in its obscure, unrecognized effects. If that great deed was what we believe it to be, what we know it is, it must remain present, though past; it must be a standing fact for all times. Our own careful reflection upon it tells us this; and therefore, when we are told that you, O Lord, though you have ascended to glory, have renewed and perpetuated your sacrifice to the end of all things, not only is the news most touching and joyful, as testifying to so tender a Lord and Savior, but it carries with it the full assent and sympathy of our reason. Though we neither could, nor would have dared, anticipate so wonderful a doctrine, yet we adore its very suitableness to your perfections, as well as its infinite compassion for us, now that we are told of it. Yes, my Lord, though you have left the world, you are daily offered up in the Mass; and, though you cannot suffer pain and death, you still subject yourself to indignity and restraint to carry out to the full your mercies toward us. You humble yourself daily; for, being infinite, you could not end your humiliation while they existed for whom you submitted to it. So you remain a priest forever.

My Lord, I offer you myself in turn as a sacrifice of thanksgiving. You have died for me, and I in turn make myself over to you. I am not my own. You have bought me; I will by my own act and deed complete the purchase. My wish is to be separated from everything of this world; to cleanse myself simply from sin; to put away from me even what is innocent, if used for its own sake, and not for yours. I put away reputation and honor, and influence, and power, for my praise and strength shall be in you. Enable me to carry out what I profess.

41

Holy Communion

My God, who can be inhabited by you, except the pure and holy? Sinners may come to you, but to whom should you come except to the sanctified? My God, I adore you as the holiest; and, when you came upon earth, you prepared a holy habitation for yourself in the most chaste womb of the Blessed Virgin. You did make a dwelling place special for yourself. She did not receive you without first being prepared for you; for from the moment that she was at all, she was filled with your grace, so that she never knew sin. And so she went on increasing in grace and merit year after year, until the time came when you sent down the archangel to signify to her your presence within her. So holy must be the dwelling place of the Highest. I adore and glorify you, O Lord my God, for your great holiness.

O my God, holiness becomes your house (cf. Ps. 93:5), and yet you make your abode in my breast. My Lord, my Savior, to me you come, hidden under the semblance of earthly things, yet in that very flesh and blood which you took from Mary. You, who first inhabited Mary's breast, come to me.

My God, you see me; I cannot see myself. Were I ever so good a judge about myself, ever so unbiased, and with ever so correct a rule of judging, still, from my very nature, I cannot look at myself, and view myself truly and wholly. But you, as you come to me, contemplate me. When I say, "Lord, I am not worthy," you whom I am addressing alone understand in their fullness the words I use. You see how unworthy so great a sinner is to receive the one holy God, whom the seraphim adore with trembling. You see, not only the stains and scars of past sins, but the mutilations, the deep cavities, the chronic disorders they have left in my soul. You see the innumerable living sins, though they be not mortal, living in their power and presence, their guilt, and their penalties, which clothe me. You see all my bad habits, all my mean principles, all wayward lawless thoughts, my multitude of infirmities and miseries, yet you come. You see most perfectly how little I really feel what I am now saying, yet you come. O my God, left to myself should I not perish under the awful splendor and the consuming fire of your Majesty? Enable me to bear you, lest I have to say with Peter, "Depart from me, for I am a sinful man, O Lord" (Luke 5:8).

Everyday Meditations

My God, enable me to bear you, for you alone can. Cleanse my heart and mind from all that is past. Wipe out clean all my recollections of evil. Rid me from all languor, sickliness, irritability, feebleness of soul. Give me a true perception of things unseen, and make me truly, practically, and in the details of life, prefer you to anything on earth, and the future world to the present. Give me courage, a true instinct determining between right and wrong, humility in all things, and a tender longing love of you.

42

The Food of the Soul

In you, O Lord, all things live, and you give them their food. *Oculi omnium in te sperant*—"The eyes of all hope in you" (Ps. 145:15). To the beasts of the field you give meat and drink. They live on day by day, because you give them day by day to live. And, if you give not, they feel their misery at once. Nature witnesses to this great truth, for they are visited at once with great agony, and they cry out and wildly wander about, seeking what they need. But, as to us your children, you feed us with another food. You know, O my God, who made us, that nothing can satisfy us but you, and therefore you have caused your own self to be meat and drink to us. O most adorable mystery! O most stupendous of mercies! You most glorious, and beautiful, and strong, and sweet, you knew well that nothing else would support our immortal natures, our frail hearts, but you; and so you took a human flesh and blood, that they, as being the flesh and blood of God, might be our life.

Oh, what an awesome thought! You deal otherwise with others, but, as to me, the flesh and blood of God is my sole life. I shall perish without it; yet shall I not perish with it and by it? How can I raise myself to such an act as to feed upon God? O my God, I am in a strait — shall I go forward, or shall I go back? I will go forward: I will go to meet you. I will open my mouth and receive your gift. I do so with great awe and fear, but what else can I do? To whom should I go but to you? Who can save me but you? Who can cleanse me but you? Who can make me overcome myself but you? Who can raise my body from the grave but you? Therefore I come to you in all these my necessities, in fear, but in faith.

My God, you are my life; if I leave you, I cannot but thirst. Lost spirits thirst in hell, because they have not God. They thirst, though they fain would have it otherwise, from the necessity of their original nature. But I, my God, wish to thirst for you with a better thirst. I wish to be clad in that new nature, which so longs for you from loving you, as to overcome in me the fear of coming to you. I come to you, O Lord, not only because I am unhappy without you, not only because I feel I need you, but because your grace draws me on to seek you for your own sake, because you are so glorious and beautiful. I come in great fear, but in greater love. Oh, may I never lose, as years pass away, and the heart shuts up, and all things are a burden, let me never lose this youthful, eager, elastic love of you. Make your grace supply the failure of nature. Do the more for me, the less I can do for myself. The more I refuse to open my heart to you, so much the fuller and stronger be your supernatural visitings, and the more urgent and efficacious your presence in me.

43

The Sacred Heart

O Sacred Heart of Jesus, I adore you in the oneness of the personality of the second person of the Holy Trinity.

Whatever belongs to the person of Jesus belongs therefore to God and is to be worshipped with that one and the same worship which we pay to Jesus. He did not take on himself his human nature as something distinct and separate from himself, but as simply, absolutely, eternally his, so as to be included by us in the very thought of him.

I worship you, O heart of Jesus, as being Jesus himself, as being that Eternal Word in human nature which he took wholly and lives in wholly, and therefore in you. You are the heart of the Most High made man. In worshipping you, I worship my incarnate God, Emmanuel. I worship you, as bearing a part in that passion which is my life, for you burst and broke, through agony, in the Garden of Gethsemane, and your precious contents trickled out, through the veins and pores of the skin, upon the earth. And again, you had been drained all but dry upon the Cross; and then, after death, you were pierced by the lance and gave out the small remains of that inestimable treasure, which is our redemption.

My God, my Savior, I adore your Sacred Heart, for that heart is the seat and source of all your tender human affections for us sinners. It is the instrument and organ of your love. It beat for us. It yearned over us. It ached for us and for our salvation. It was on fire through zeal, that the glory of God might be manifested in and by us. It is the channel through which has come to us all your overflowing human affection, all your divine charity toward us. All your incomprehensible compassion for us, as God and Man, as our Creator and our Redeemer and Judge, has come to us, and comes, in one inseparably mingled stream, through that Sacred Heart. O most sacred symbol and sacrament of love, divine and human, in its fullness, you saved me by your divine strength, and your human affection and then at length by that wonder-working blood, wherewith you overflowed.

O most sacred, most loving Heart of Jesus, you are concealed in the Holy Eucharist, and you beat for us still. Now as then you say, "With desire I have desired" (Luke 22:15). I worship you then with all my best love and awe, with my fervent affection, with my most subdued, most resolved will. O my God, when you condescend to suffer me to receive you, to eat and drink you, and you for a while take up your abode within me, make my heart beat with your heart. Purify it of all that is earthly, all that is proud and sensual, all that is hard and cruel, of all perversity, of all disorder, of all deadness. So fill it with you, that neither the events of the day nor the circumstances of the time may have power to ruffle it but that in your love and your fear it may have peace.

44

The Infinite Perfection of God

Ex ipso, et per ipsum, et in ipso sunt omnia.

Ex ipso. I adore you, O my God, as the origin and source of all that is in the world. Once nothing was in being but you. It was so for a whole eternity. You alone have had no beginning. You have ever been in being without beginning. You have necessarily been a whole eternity by yourself, having in you all perfections stored up in yourself, by yourself; a world of worlds; an infinite abyss of all that is great and wonderful, beautiful and holy; a treasury of infinite attributes, all in one; infinitely one while thus infinitely various.

My God, the thought simply exceeds a created nature, much more mine. I cannot attain to it; I can but use the words, and say, "I believe" without comprehending. But this I can do: I can adore you, O my great and good God, as the one source of all perfection, and that I do, and with your grace will do always.

Per ipsum. And when other beings began to be, they lived through you. They did not begin of themselves. They did not come into existence except by your determinate will, by your eternal counsel, by your sole operation. They are wholly from you. From eternity, in the deep ocean of your blessedness, you predestinated everything which in its hour took place. Not a substance, even one ever so insignificant, is not of your design and your work. Much more, not a soul comes into being but by your direct appointment and act. You see, you have seen from all eternity, every individual of your creatures.

You have seen me, O my God, from all eternity. You see distinctly, and ever have seen, whether I am to be saved or to be lost. You see my history through all ages in heaven or in hell. O awful thought! My God, enable me to bear it, lest the thought of you confound me utterly. And lead me forward to salvation.

In ipso. And I believe and know, moreover, that all things live in you. Whatever there is of being, of life, of excellence, of enjoyment, of happiness, in the whole creation, is, in its substance, simply and absolutely yours. It is by dipping into the ocean of your infinite perfections that all beings have whatever they have of good. All the beauty and majesty of the visible world is a shadow or a glimpse of you, or the manifestation or operation in a created medium of one or another of your attributes. All that is wonderful in the way of talent or genius is but an unworthy reflection of the faintest gleam of the eternal mind. Whatever we do well is not only by your help, but is after all scarcely an imitation of that sanctity which is in fullness in you.

O my God, shall I one day see you? What sight can compare to that great sight! Shall I see the source of that grace which enlightens me, strengthens me, and consoles me? As I came from you, as I am made through you, as I live in you, so, O my God, may I at last return to you and be with you forever and ever.

45

The Infinite Knowledge of God

All things are naked and open to his eyes; neither is there any creature invisible in his sight (Heb. 4:13).

God, I adore you, as beholding all things. You know in a way altogether different from and higher than any knowledge that can belong to creatures. We know by means of sight and thought; there are few things we know in any other way; but how unlike this knowledge, not only in extent, but in its nature and its characteristics, is your knowledge! The angels know many things, but their knowledge compared with yours is mere ignorance. The human soul, which you took into yourself when you became man, was filled from the first with all the knowledge possible to human nature; but even that was nothing but a drop compared with the abyss of that knowledge, and its keen luminousness, which is yours as God.

My God, could it be otherwise? From the first and from everlasting you were by yourself; and your blessedness consisted in knowing and contemplating yourself, the Father in the Son and Spirit, and the Son and Spirit severally in each other and in the Father, thus infinitely comprehending the infinite. If you knew your infinite self thus perfectly, you knew that which was greater and more than anything else could be. All that the whole universe contains, put together, is after all but finite. It is finite, though it be illimitable! It is finite, though it be so multiform; it is finite, though it be so marvelously skillful, beautiful, and magnificent; but you are the infinite God, and, knowing yourself, much more do you know the whole universe, however vast, however intricate and various, and all that is in it.

My great God, you know all that is in the universe, because you yourself have made it. It is the very work of your hands. You are omniscient, because you are omnicreative. You know each part, however minute, as perfectly as you know the whole. You know mind as perfectly as you know matter. You know the thoughts and purposes of every soul as perfectly as if there were no other soul in the whole of your creation. You know me through and through; all my present, past, and future are before you as one whole. You see all those delicate and evanescent motions of my thought which altogether escape myself. You can trace every act, whether deed or thought, to its origin and can follow it into its whole growth and consequences. You know how it will be with me at the end; you have before you that hour when I shall come to you to be judged. How awful is the prospect of finding myself in the presence of my judge! Yet, O Lord, I would not that you should not know me. It is my greatest stay to know that you read my heart. Oh, give me more of that openhearted sincerity which I have desired. Keep me ever from being afraid of your eye, from the inward consciousness that I am not honestly trying to please you. Teach me to love you more, and then I shall be at peace, without any fear of you at all.

46

The Providence of God

I adore you, my God, as having laid down the ends and the means of all things you have created. You have created everything for some end of its own, and you direct it to that end. The end that you appointed for man in the beginning is your worship and service and his own happiness in paying it; a blessed eternity of soul and body with you forever. You have provided for this, and that in the case of every man.

As your hand and eye are upon the brute creation, so are they upon us. You sustain everything in life and action for its own end. Not a reptile, not an insect you do not see and make to live, while its time lasts. Not a sinner, not an idolater, not a blasphemer, not an atheist lives but by you and in order that he may repent. You are careful and tender to each of the beings you have created, as if it were the only one in the whole world. For you can see every one of them at once, and you love every one in this mortal life, and pursue every one by itself, with all the fullness of your attributes, as if you were waiting on it and ministering to it for its own sake. My God, I love to contemplate you, I love to adore you, thus the wonderful worker of all things every day in every place.

All your acts of providence are acts of love. If you send evil upon us, it is in love. All the evils of the physical world are intended for the good of your creatures or are the unavoidable attendants on that good. And you turn that evil into good. You visit men with evil to bring them to repentance, to increase their virtue, to gain for them greater good hereafter. Nothing is done in vain, but has its gracious end. You punish, yet in wrath you remember mercy. Even your justice, when it overtakes the impenitent sinner, who had exhausted your loving providences toward him, is mercy to others, as saving them from his contamination or granting them a warning. I acknowledge with a full and firm faith, O Lord, the wisdom and goodness of your providence, even in your inscrutable judgments and your incomprehensible decrees.

O my God, my whole life has been a course of mercies and blessings shown to one who has been most unworthy of them. I require no faith, for I have had long experience as to your providence toward me. Year after year you have carried me on—removed dangers from my path—recovered me, recruited me, refreshed me, borne with me, directed me, sustained me. Oh, forsake me not when my strength fails me. And you never will forsake me. I may securely repose upon you. Sinner as I am, nevertheless, while I am true to you, you will still, and to the end, be superabundantly true to me.

I may rest upon your arm; I may go to sleep in your bosom. Only give me, and increase in me, that true loyalty to you which is the bond of the covenant between you and me and the pledge in my own heart and conscience that you, the Supreme God, will not forsake me, the most miserable of your children.

47

God Is All in All

One God and Father of all, who is above all, and through all, and in us all (Eph. 4:6).

God alone is in heaven; God is all in all. Eternal Lord, I acknowledge this truth, and I adore you in this sovereign and most glorious mystery. There is one God, and he fills heaven; and all blessed creatures, though they ever remain in their individuality, are, as the very means of their blessedness, absorbed, and (as it were) drowned in the fullness of him who is *super omnes, et per omnia, et in omnibus.*

If ever, through your grace, I attain to see you in heaven, I shall see nothing else but you, because I shall see all whom I see in you, and seeing them I shall see you. As I cannot see things here below without light, and to see them is to see the rays that come from them, so in that eternal city *claritas Dei illuminavit eam, et lucerna eius est agnus* — "the glory of God hath enlightened it, and the

Lamb is the lamp thereof" (Rev. 21:23). My God, I adore you now (at least I will do so to the best of my powers) as the one sole true life and light of the soul, as I shall know and see you to be hereafter, if by your grace I attain to heaven.

Eternal, incomprehensible God, I believe and confess and adore you as being infinitely more wonderful, resourceful, and immense than this universe which I see. I look into the depths of space, in which the stars are scattered about, and I understand that I would be millions upon millions of years in creeping along from one end of it to the other, if a bridge were thrown across it. I consider the overpowering variety, richness, and intricacy of your work; the elements, the principles, the laws, and the results that go to make it up. I try to recount the multitudes of kinds of knowledge, of sciences, and of arts of which it can be made the subject. And, I know, I would be ages upon ages in learning everything that is to be learned about this world, supposing me to have the power of learning it at all. And new sciences would come to light, at present unsuspected, as fast as I had mastered the old, and the conclusions of today would be nothing more than starting points of tomorrow. And I see moreover, and the more I examined it, the more I should understand, the marvelous beauty of these works of your

Everyday Meditations

hands. And so, I might begin again, after this material universe, and find a new world of knowledge, higher and more wonderful, in your intellectual creations, your angels and other spirits, and men. But all, all that is in these worlds, high and low, are but an atom compared with the grandeur, the height and depth, the glory, on which your saints are gazing in their contemplation of you. It is the occupation of eternity, ever new, inexhaustible, ineffably ecstatic, the stay and the blessedness of existence, thus to drink in and be dissolved in you.

My God, it was your supreme blessedness in the eternity past, as it is your blessedness in all eternities, to know yourself, as you alone can know you. It was by seeing yourself in your coequal Son and your coeternal Spirit, and in their seeing you, that Father, Son, and Holy Spirit, three persons, one God, was infinitely blessed. O my God, what am I that you should make my blessedness to consist in that which is your own! That you should grant me to have not only the sight of you, but to share in your very own joy! O prepare me for it, teach me to thirst for it.

48

The Incommunicable Perfection of God

Almighty God, you are the one infinite fullness. From eternity you are the one and only absolute and most all-sufficient seat and proper abode of all conceivable best attributes and of all, which are many more, that cannot be conceived. I hold this as a matter of reason, though my imagination starts from it. I hold it firmly and absolutely, though it is the most difficult of all mysteries. I hold it from the actual experience of your blessings and mercies toward me, the evidences of your awesome being and attributes, brought home continually to my reason, beyond the power of doubting or disputing. I hold it from that long and intimate familiarity with it, so that it is part of my rational nature to hold it; because I am so constituted and made up upon the idea of it, as a keystone, that not to hold it would be to break my mind to pieces. I hold it from that intimate perception of it in my conscience, as a fact present to me, that I feel it as easy to deny my own personality as the personality of God, and have lost my grounds for believing that I exist myself, if I deny existence to him. I hold it because I could not bear to be without you, O my Lord and life, because I look for blessings beyond thought by being with you. I hold it from the terror of being left in this wild world without stay or protection. I hold it from humble love to you, from delight in your glory and exaltation, from my desire that you should be great and the only great one. I hold it for your sake and because I love to think of you as so glorious, perfect, and beautiful. There is one God, and none other but he.

Since, O eternal God, you are so incommunicably great, so one, so perfect in that oneness, surely one would say, you ever must be most distant from your creatures, separated from them by your eternal ancientness on their beginning to be, and separated by your transcendence of excellence and your absolute contrariety to them. What could you give them out of yourself that would suit their nature, so different from yours? What good of yours could be their good, or do them good, except in some poor external way? If you could be the happiness of man, then might man in turn, or some gift from him, be the happiness of the bird of prey or the wild beast, the cattle of his pasture, or the myriads of minute creatures we can scarcely see? Man is not so far above them, as you are above him. For what is every creature in your sight, O Lord, but a vanity and a breath, a smoke that stays not, but flits by and passes away, a poor thing that only vanishes so much the sooner, because you look on it and it is set in the illumination of your countenance? Is not this, O Lord, the perplexity of reason? From the perfect comes the perfect; yet you cannot make a second God, from the nature of the case; and therefore either cannot create at all, or of necessity must create what is infinitely unlike, and therefore, in a sense, unworthy of the Creator.

What communion then can there be between you and me? O my God! What am I but a parcel of dead bones, a feeble, tottering, miserable being, compared with you? I am your work, and you created me pure from sin, but how can you look upon me in my best estate of nature, with complacency? How can you see in me any image of yourself, the Creator? How is this, my Lord? You pronounced your work very good and made man in your image. Yet there is an infinite gulf between you and me, O my God.

49

God Communicated to Us

You have, O Lord, an incommunicable perfection, but still that omnipotence by which you created is sufficient also to the work of communicating yourself to the spirits you have created. Your almighty life is not for our destruction, but for our living. You remain ever one and the same in yourself, but there goes from you continually a power and virtue that by its contact is our strength and good. I do not know how this can be; my reason does not satisfy me here; but in nature I see intimations, and by faith I have full assurance of the truth of this mystery. By you we cross the gulf that lies between you and us. The living God is lifegiving. You are the fount and center, as well as the seat, of all good. The traces of your glory, as the many-colored rays of the sun, are scattered over the whole face of nature, without diminution of your perfections, or violation of your transcendent and unapproachable essence. How it can be, I know not; but so it is. And thus, remaining one and sole and infinitely removed from all things, still you are the fullness of all things; in you they consist, of you they partake, and into you, retaining their own individuality, they are absorbed. And thus, while we droop and decay in our own nature, we live by your breath; and your grace enables us to endure your presence.

Make me then like yourself, O my God, since, in spite of myself, such you can make me, such I can be made. Look on me, O my Creator, pity the work of your hands; let me not perish in my infirmity. Take me out of my natural imbecility, since that is possible for me, which is so necessary. You have shown it to be possible in the face of the whole world by the most overwhelming proof, by taking our created nature on yourself, and exalting it in you. Give me in my own self the benefit of this wondrous truth, now that it has been so publicly ascertained and guaranteed. Let me have in my own person what in Jesus you have given to my nature. Let me be partaker of that divine nature in all the riches of its attributes, which in fullness of substance and in personal presence became the Son of Mary. Give me that life, suitable to my own need, which is stored up for us all in him who is the life of men. Teach me and enable me to live the life of saints and angels. Take me out of the languor, the irritability, the sensitiveness, the incapability, the anarchy, in which my soul lies, and fill it with your fullness. Breathe on me, that the dead bones may live. Breathe on me with that breath which infuses energy and kindles fervor.

In asking for fervor, I ask for all that I can need, and all that you can give; for it is the crown of all gifts and all virtues. It cannot really and fully be, except where all are at present. It is the beauty and the glory, as it is also the continual safeguard and purifier of them all. In asking for fervor, I am asking for effectual strength, consistency, and perseverance. I am asking for deadness to every human motive and for simplicity of intention to please you. I am asking for faith, hope, and charity in their most heavenly exercise. In asking for fervor I am asking to be rid of the fear of man, and the desire of his praise. I am asking for the gift of prayer, because it will be so sweet. I am asking for that loyal perception of duty which follows on yearning affection. I am asking for sanctity, peace, and joy all at once. In asking for fervor, I am asking for the brightness of the cherubim and the fire of the seraphim, and the whiteness of all saints. In asking for fervor, I am asking for that which, while it implies all gifts, is that in which I signally fail. Nothing would be a trouble to me, nothing a difficulty, had I but fervor of soul.

Lord, in asking for fervor, I am asking for yourself, for nothing short of you, O my God, who have given yourself wholly to us. Enter my heart substantially and personally, and fill it with fervor by filling it with you. You alone can fill the soul of man, and you have promised to do so. You are the living flame, and ever burn with love of man: enter into me and set me on fire after your pattern and likeness.

50

God Is the Sole Stay for Eternity

My God I believe and know and adore you as infinite in the multiplicity and depth of your attributes. I adore you as containing in you an abundance of all that can delight and satisfy the soul.

I know, on the contrary, and from sad experience I am too sure, that whatever is created, whatever is earthly, pleases but for the time and then palls and is a weariness. I believe that there is nothing at all here below that I would not at length get sick of. I believe, that, though I had all the means of happiness that this life could give, yet in time I would tire of living, feeling everything trite and dull and unprofitable. I believe, that, were it my lot to live the long antediluvian life, and to live it without you, I would be utterly, inconceivably wretched at the end of it. I think I would be tempted to destroy myself for very weariness and disgust. I think I would at last lose my reason and go mad, if my life here were prolonged long enough. I would feel it like solitary confinement, for I would find myself shut up in myself without companion, if I could not converse with you, my God. You only, O my infinite Lord, are ever new, though you are the ancient of days — the last as well as the first.

You, O my God, are ever new, though you are the most ancient — you alone are the food for eternity. I am to live forever, not for a time, and I have no power over my being. I cannot destroy myself, even if I were so wicked as to wish to do so. I must live on, with intellect and consciousness forever, in spite of myself. Without you eternity would be another name for eternal misery. In you alone have I that which can stay me up forever: you alone are the food of my soul. You alone are inexhaustible, and ever offer to me something new to know, something new to love. At the end of millions of years, I shall know you so little that I shall seem to myself only beginning. At the end of millions of years I shall find in you the same, or rather, greater sweetness than at first and shall seem then only to be beginning to enjoy you: and so on for eternity I shall ever be a little child beginning to be taught the rudiments of your infinite divine nature. For you are yourself the seat and center of all good, and the only substance in this universe of shadows, and the heaven in which blessed spirits live and rejoice.

Everyday Meditations

My God, I take you for my portion. From mere pru-
dence I turn from the world to you; I give up the world
for you. I renounce that which promises for him who per-
forms. To whom else would I go? I desire to find and feed
on you here. I desire to feed on you, Jesus, my Lord, who
are risen, who have gone up on high, who yet remain
with your people on earth. I look up to you. I look for
the living bread which is in heaven, which comes down
from heaven. Give me ever of this bread. Destroy this
life, which will soon perish, even though you do not destroy it, and fill me with that supernatural life, which will
never die.

An Invitation

Reader, the book that you hold in your hands was published by Sophia Institute Press.

Sophia Institute seeks to restore man's knowledge of eternal truth, including man's knowledge of his own nature, his relation to other persons, and his relation to God.

Our press fulfills this mission by offering translations, reprints, and new publications. We offer scholarly as well as popular publications; there are works of fiction along with books that draw from all the arts and sciences of our civilization. These books afford readers a rich source of the enduring wisdom of mankind.

Sophia Institute Press also serves as the publisher for the Thomas More College of Liberal Arts and Holy Spirit College. Both colleges are dedicated to providing university-level education in the Western tradition under the guiding light of Catholic teaching.

If you know a young person who might be interested in the ideas found in this book, share it. If you know a young person seeking a college that takes seriously the adventure of learning and the quest for truth, bring our institutions to his attention.

www.SophiaInstitute.com
www.ThomasMoreCollege.edu
www.HolySpiritCollege.org

SOPHIA INSTITUTE PRESS

THE PUBLISHING DIVISION OF